Saint Joseph
CONCISE BIBLE HISTORY

THE LAND OF THE BIBLE

SAINT JOSEPH

CONCISE
BIBLE HISTORY

A CLEAR AND READABLE ACCOUNT
OF THE HISTORY OF SALVATION

Illustrated

Dedicated to ST. JOSEPH
Patron of the Universal Church

CATHOLIC BOOK PUBLISHING CORP.
NEW JERSEY

NIHIL OBSTAT: Daniel V. Flynn, J.C.D.

Censor Librorum

IMPRIMATUR: ✠ James P. Mahoney, D.D.

Vicar General, Archdiocese of New York

(T-770)

www.catholicbookpublishing.com

ISBN 978-0-89942-770-6

PREFACE

This new *Concise Bible History* is intended to meet the sorely felt need for a clear and readable bird's-eye view of the History of Salvation. It is not meant to supplant the Bible but to lead to a desire for a greater knowledge of the Scripture texts themselves.

By utilizing this handy volume, the reader will get a good idea of the scope of sacred history, the sequence of the major events in that history, the meaning it has for us, and the spiritual riches that can be found therein.

A large amount of material has been condensed into a compact easy-to-manage volume. The format is clear and easy-to-follow and the large print is a joy to read. The illustrations transport the reader back to the very midst of biblical times.

This all adds up to a primer on the Bible that can be of immense help to many Catholics in this age of widespread study of the Word of God.

Consequently, the present volume can be used for many purposes: as an introduction to the complete Bible by the individual person, as a text book in religion classes by elementary and high schools, and as a basic text by parish study groups.

It is the fervent hope of the publishers that this little volume will contribute in some way to the interest in and love for the Sacred Scriptures that was inaugurated by the Biblical Movement, fostered by our great modern Popes, and strongly encouraged by the Second Vatican Council.

CONTENTS

PART I: THE OLD TESTAMENT

PART II: THE LIFE OF JESUS

I. Birth and Early Life

II. Public Ministry

III. Passion, Death, and Resurrection

PART III: THE EARLY CHURCH

MAPS

God the Creator of heaven and earth, and of all things.

THE OLD TESTAMENT

THE CREATION

THE Bible tells us that God made the world out of nothing in six days, or periods of time. All was empty and dark. Then the breath of God moved over the waters.

On the first day, God created light, and He divided the light and darkness into day and night. God saw that it was good.

On the second day, God made the heavens and divided the waters under the heavens from those above. He called the heavens "the sky."

On the third day, God separated the dry land from the waters under the sky. He called the dry land "the earth" and the waters "the sea," and He saw that it was good. He also made different kinds of trees and plants which would give seed and fruit, each according to its own kind. God saw that this too was good.

On the fourth day, God made the heavenly bodies to shine in the sky. These would give signs and be measures of time for seasons and days and years. The sun was to rule the day, and the moon and stars were to shine at night. God saw that this was good.

On the fifth day, God made the fish and all the creatures that would live in the waters. He also made the fowl and the birds of the air. He blessed these creatures and gave them the power to increase and multiply. And God saw that all these were good.

On the sixth day, God made all the animals and creeping things that move on the earth. And He saw that this was good. Then He made man from the dust of the earth. He created them according to His own image, both male and female. He blessed them and gave them power to increase and multiply and to rule over the earth and all living creatures.

God saw that everything He had created was very good, and He rested on the seventh day, which He blessed and made holy because the work of His creation was finished.

THE EARTHLY PARADISE

God planted a large and beautiful garden, called **Eden**, in which grew all kinds of trees and plants, and the animals roamed through it. Here He placed the first man, Adam. God told Adam to take command over the beasts and flying creatures, and Adam gave names to them all. Then one day while Adam slept, God took out one of his ribs and from this He formed a woman, and filled in the vacant space with flesh.

God told Adam and Eve that they might eat of all the fruit except the Tree of Knowledge which grew in the middle of the garden. If they ate the fruit of this tree, they would surely die. But one day, the serpent, the most cunning of all the creatures, told Eve to eat this fruit. She did so and gave some to Adam, who ate it also. Because they disobeyed God's command, they were driven from the Garden of Eden and were doomed to labor, to suffer and to die. God also condemned the serpent to crawl on the ground and eat dust all the days of its life.

God told Adam and Eve that they would return to the ground from which they had been created: "For you are dust, and to dust you shall return." God then provided them with clothing and sent them out to labor, and set His Cherubim before the garden with a sword of fire to prevent Adam and Eve from eating the fruit of the tree of life. God did not, however, abandon Adam and Eve, but promised them a Redeemer, who would save the human race.

CAIN AND ABEL

Cain and Abel were two sons of Adam and Eve. Cain was a farmer and Abel was a shepherd. Both offered sacrifice to

God, but with very different dispositions. Because Abel's disposition was good God loved him, and Cain became jealous of his brother. One day when they were in the fields, Cain killed Abel. God punished Cain by condemning him to roam over the earth. Cain became the father of a race of wicked people, called the "children of men."

Adam and Eve had another son, born after the murder of Abel, whom they called **Seth**. The descendants of Seth were known for their piety and are called the "sons of heaven." However, they soon began to mingle with the race of Cain and became corrupt like the rest. So great was their wickedness that there could be found little virtue in them.

THE DELUGE

When God saw how evil men had become, He told Noah, who was a very holy man, to build a large ship and He gave Noah the measurements and directions for building this ark. After many years the ark was completed, and Noah, with all his family and two of every kind of animal, went into the ark. Then all the people and all living things on the earth perished in a great deluge. At the end of a year, Noah came out of the ark with his family and all the animals he had taken into it. Immediately he offered a sacrifice in thanksgiving to God for the favor bestowed on him and his family. God was pleased with this offering and promised that He would not destroy the earth again in this way. He set His rainbow in the sky as a sign of this promise.

Then Noah and his three sons, Shem, Ham and Japheth, began to cultivate the earth. Mankind soon increased in number and all lived in the same place and spoke the same language. Men then decided among themselves to build a city and a tower which would reach the sky.

But because of their pride and lack of faith, God punished them by changing their language so that they could not understand one another. He scattered them throughout the world and they were unable to finish building their city and tower, which was called **Babel**, because of the confusion of language.

ABRAHAM

Abraham, or Abram, as he was called was a just and holy man who lived with his family in the country of the Chaldees. When he was 75 years old, God told him to leave his own country and to go into the land of Canaan, which He said He would give to Abram and his descendants. God also blessed Abram and promised to make a great nation of him. Abram did all that God told him and departed for Canaan, taking his nephew Lot and his family with him.

Abram and his family depart for the land of Canaan.

Lot Is Rescued

A dispute arose on the way between Abram's and Lot's servants, so they agreed to separate. After this, Lot was taken prisoner by the king of the Elamites and Abram rescued him. On his way home, Abram was blessed by Melchizedek, king of Salem and a priest of God, who offered sacrifice of bread and wine. When Abram was 99 years old, God changed his name to Abraham, which means "father of many nations."

Birth of Isaac

In a year's time Sarah gave birth to a son, whom they called Isaac. The birth of Isaac had been foretold by God and two angels who had visited Abraham. When he was eight days old, Isaac was circumcised, in accordance with God's command to Abraham that every male child among the Jews should be circumcised.

Sodom

About this time fire from heaven destroyed the cities of Sodom and Gomorrah because of their wickedness. But Lot and his family were saved by the angels who had visited Abraham.

In the meantime Isaac grew up in the care of his parents. One day, Sarah saw Ishmael, Abraham's son by the slave-girl, Hagar, mocking her son. She asked Abraham to send Hagar and her son away. The Patriarch very reluctantly consented to do this.

Abraham's Sacrifice

In order to test him, God commanded Abraham to sacrifice his only son Isaac. As he was about to slay him, God sent an angel to stop him. Abraham then found a ram which he sacrificed instead. This was the greatest proof of Abraham's faith. St. Paul speaks of him as "Faithful Abraham" and as the "Friend of God."

ISAAC

After the death of Sarah, Isaac married his cousin Rebekah, daughter of Abraham's kinsman from his own country. Abraham died at the age of 175 years and Isaac and Ishmael buried him beside Sarah in the double cave in the field of Ephron, near Mamre. The chief part of Abraham's property was left to Isaac. Two sons were born to Isaac when he was about sixty years old. The older boy he called Esau because he was covered with red hair. The younger son was called Jacob. Isaac loved Esau, while Jacob was his mother's favorite.

ESAU AND JACOB

Esau was a skillful hunter, but Jacob loved to tend his flocks. When Isaac was about to give his blessing, he sent Esau out to bring him some venison. Isaac was nearly blind, and while Esau was out, Rebekah obtained the blessing for Jacob by dressing him in his brother's clothes and preparing a dish of venison for him to take to his father. Esau had already sold his birthright to Jacob for a portion of food when he was hungry.

Jacob's Flight

When Esau found out that Jacob had received their father's blessing intended for himself, he became very angry and Jacob had to flee to Mesopotamia. During his journey Jacob had a vision in which God promised him the land on which he was lying, and that from him the Messiah would come.

Jacob dreams of a ladder between heaven and earth.

Jacob at Laban's

Jacob arrived at his uncle Laban's house, who was his mother's brother. There he was hired to mind the flocks and herds. After working there for some years, Jacob received Laban's permission to marry his two daughters. So he first married Leah and then Rachel and had twelve sons by them. These sons, with the exception of Levi and Joseph, became heads of the tribes of Israel. The sons were: Reuben, Simeon, Levi, Judah, Dan, Naphtali, Issachar, Zebulun, Gad, Asher, Joseph and Benjamin.

Jacob's Return

After twenty years, Jacob left Laban's house with his wives and children to return to the land of Canaan. During this journey Jacob had a dream in which he wrestled with an angel whom he overcame. On this occasion his name was changed to **Israel**. The next day he was reconciled with his brother Esau. Upon his return to Canaan, Jacob bought a piece of land where he encamped, and built an altar there which he dedicated to the almighty God, the God of Israel.

Dinah

While Dinah, the daughter of Jacob and Leah, was visiting in that country, one of the princes of the Shechemites defiled her. Jacob's sons took the city of these people by surprise and killed all the inhabitants. This deed of blood was bitterly lamented by Jacob.

Death of Rachel

Soon after this massacre of the Shechemites, Rachel died and was buried at Bethlehem. Isaac also died about this time, having reached the age of 185 years.

JOSEPH

Of all their sons, Jacob and Rachel loved Joseph best. Because of this and the special favors bestowed on him, his brothers became jealous. Joseph was a most devoted and affectionate son to his parents.

His Dreams

Joseph had two dreams: (1) that the sun, moon, and eleven stars worshiped him; (2) that his brothers' sheaves of corn bowed down before his. On hearing this, the brothers determined to kill him, but Reuben persuaded them not to shed blood. Instead, at Judah's suggestion, they sold him to a band of Ishmaelites, who carried him off to Egypt to the house of Potiphar, an officer of the Pharaoh. He was soon thrown into prison through the lies of Potiphar's wife, who wanted him to commit sin.

Interprets Dreams

In the prison with Joseph were Pharaoh's chief baker and chief butler, whose dreams he interpreted. When Joseph had been in prison about two years, Pharaoh had a dream in which he saw seven lean cows devouring seven fat ones, and seven full ears of corn spoiled by seven blighted ones. Joseph was sent for and interpreted these dreams by foretelling seven

Pharaoh puts a chain of gold around Joseph's neck.

years of plenty in the land, to be followed by seven years of famine. Pharaoh then made him chief minister.

In Power

During the years of plenty, Joseph saw to it that as much of the corn as could be spared was bound in sheaves and stored in various storehouses in Egypt. When the famine came and Jacob's sons heard that corn could be bought in Egypt, they came there to buy provisions, but they did not know Joseph. However, he recognized his brothers. At their third visit he revealed himself to them and told them to bring their father and their families and settle there.

Death of Jacob

Jacob had been given the land of Goshen by Pharaoh, where he lived to the time of his death at the age of 147 years. On his deathbed he gave a special blessing to each of his sons.

Death of Joseph

Joseph died at the age of 110 years, leaving two sons, Ephraim and Manasseh, who became the heads of two of the twelve tribes of Israel.

MOSES AND THE DELIVERANCE

Many years after the death of Joseph, the Hebrews had become so numerous that a new king determined to oppress them in order to prevent them from becoming too powerful. So he commanded his overseers to make them do all the hard work in the country. But since this law did not have the desired effect, the king ordered all their male children to be drowned in the river Nile as soon as they wore born.

Birth of Moses

About this time, Moses, the son of one of the tribe of Levi, was born. His mother kept him hidden for three months after which she placed him on the banks of the river in a cradle made of rushes.

When Pharaoh's daughter went to the river to bathe, she noticed the basket and sent her handmaid to fetch it. She recognized the baby as belonging to one of the Hebrew women. Her maid, who was the baby's sister, called a Hebrew woman as a nurse for the boy. This was the baby's own mother who took care of him. When he was old enough she brought him to Pharaoh's daughter who adopted him as her own son, giving him the name of Moses because he had been rescued from the water.

His Flight

When Moses was forty years old he saw an Egyptian kill a Hebrew. Moses killed the Egyptian and buried his body in the sand. But this was soon found out and Moses fled to the land of Midian. He stayed there with Jethro for forty years and married one of his daughters called Zipporah.

His Vocation

One day when he was minding Jethro's flocks and had led them to Mount Horeb, an angel appeared to him in a burning bush. Moses noticed that while the bush was on fire, it was not consumed, so he went over to examine it. But God spoke

God speaks to Moses out of the burning bush.

to him from that burning bush, ordering him to remove his sandals because he was on holy ground. God told Moses who He was and then gave him the mission to deliver His oppressed people from the Egyptians. His brother Aaron was appointed as his companion and assistant, and God promised to help them both in speaking to the people.

God then told Moses that He would be with him and that when He brought the Israelites out of Egypt, they were to worship Him on that very mountain. God worked many miracles before Moses and Aaron.

Plagues of Egypt

The king of Egypt refused to let the Israelites go with Moses. Instead, he increased their burdens. Then God told Moses that He would send plagues on the people of Egypt through him and Aaron. The following are the ten plagues inflicted on the Egyptians:

(1) The water turned into blood. (2) Frogs overran the countryside. (3) Gnats came upon men and animals. (4) Swarms of flies filled the houses of the Egyptians, and only the land of Goshen where the Israelites lived was spared. (5) A pestilence killed all the animals except those of the Israelites. (6) Dust covered Egypt and caused ulcers on men and beasts. (7) Hailstones killed men, animals and all growing things. (8) A swarm of locusts ate up all vegetables and fruits. (9) Dense darkness covered Egypt for three days. (10) Death struck all the firstborn of the Egyptians.

The Passover

Before sending the tenth plague, God told Moses and Aaron that every Hebrew family must sacrifice a lamb and eat it with unleavened bread and herbs. They were to eat this meal standing, as if ready to go on a journey. The blood of the lamb they were to sprinkle on their doorposts. This meal would be called the "Passover," because the Lord passed over

The destroying angel passes by the house of the Israelites.

the houses of the Israelites when He killed all the firstborn of the Egyptians. The Israelites were then allowed to leave Egypt after being in that land 400 years.

The Red Sea

While they were camping on the shores of the Red Sea, the Hebrews saw the Egyptian army, led by the king, coming to attack them. God told Moses to stretch his rod over the water, which immediately parted, leaving a dry passage for them to march through. After they had crossed to safety, the Egyptians followed them. But God caused the water to flow back and all the Egyptians were drowned.

THE ISRAELITES IN THE DESERT

After crossing the Red Sea, the Israelites traveled through the desert for three days without finding water. When they arrived at Marah, they came upon a fountain, but they could not drink the water because it was bitter. The people began to grumble and so God ordered Moses to throw the branch of a tree into the water, which he did. At once the water became fresh. From Marah, they marched to Elim, where there were twelve fountains and seventy palm trees. By this time all the provisions they had brought from Egypt were consumed.

Manna and Quail

The people complained to Moses of their hunger, so Moses prayed to God. God heard his prayer and sent them manna, which fell from the sky every morning, enough for each day's needs. In the evening, quail covered the camp, so they had flesh to eat. The manna was like white hoarfrost and Moses told them it was the bread which the Lord was giving them to eat. This bread was supplied to them during the forty years they spent in the desert. It is a type of the Holy Eucharist.

Rock of Horeb

When the Israelites reached Mount Horeb, they encamped there. Again there was no water, so God told Moses to strike the rock with his rod. As soon as he did so, water flowed out in abundance, and the people stopped their murmuring. This place was called Massah and Meribah, because it was there that the Israelites quarreled and tested the Lord.

Defeat of Amalek

The first people to make war upon the Israelites were the Amalekites. Joshua was chosen to lead the Israelites in battle against these enemies. Moses, Aaron and Hur went to the top of Mount Horeb to pray. As long as Moses kept his arms raised in prayer the battle went in Israel's favor, but whenever he lowered his arms their enemies got the better of them. As Moses' arms grew tired, Aaron and Hur supported him, one on either side, until sundown when Israel was victorious. This is an example of the power of prayer when we ask God to help us. Soon after this battle, Moses appointed a number of judges to help him in governing the people.

Mount Sinai

After fifty days, the Israelites came to Mount Sinai. Here on the mountain God gave the Ten Commandments to Moses, written on two tablets of stone. Moses stayed another forty days on the mountain. In the meantime, the people had persuaded Aaron to make a gold calf for them to worship. When Moses came down from the mountain and saw the people adoring the idol, he became so angry at their wickedness that he broke the two stone tablets.

Moses breaks the tablets of the Law.

Then Moses destroyed the gold calf and commanded that all those who continued in idolatry were to be put to death. About 3,000 people perished at the hands of the Levites, who gathered round Moses. The people repented and Moses implored God to forgive their sins. The Lord in His mercy pardoned them. Then God told Moses to lead the people to the land which He had promised to Abraham, and sent His angel before them.

The Tabernacle

God ordered a Tabernacle to be made, in which He would dwell constantly in the midst of His people. This Tabernacle, or Tent, was divided into two parts: (1) the **Holy of Holies,** which contained the Ark of the Covenant; within the Ark were placed the two new stone tablets on which the Lord had written the Ten Commandments, or **Decalogue,** as they were called, together with Aaron's rod and a pot of manna; (2) the **Holy Place,** in which were the Gold Candlestick, the Table of Showbread, and the Altar of Incense; the Bronze Laver and the Altar of Holocausts were placed in front of the Holy Place. The materials were supplied through the free gifts of the people. This Tabernacle was built just two years after their departure from Egypt.

Aaron and the Priests

After the erection of the Tabernacle, Moses set apart the tribe of Levi, as the Lord had commanded, for its service. Aaron was consecrated High Priest. Then God instructed Moses in detail as to the offerings which were to be made to Him. God dwelt with His people in a cloud which hung over the Tabernacle. When the cloud was lifted, the people continued on their journey; but when it did not rise, they stayed where they were. In the daytime the people could see the cloud over the dwelling-place, but at night it was lighted by fire.

Laws of Legal Sanctity

God told Moses to teach the people to obey the laws He gave them regarding external sanctity. These laws were to show that they belonged to the Lord. Often they were reminded that they must be holy because the Lord, their God, is holy.

Numbering the People

God ordered Moses to number the people before leaving Mount Sinai. This he did, dividing the twelve tribes and registering each male individually.

Election of Ancients

When the people began to complain again, Moses asked God what he should do. So God told him to choose seventy

On the right is pictured the Tabernacle or Dwelling built according to God's specifications to Moses. In the court of the Tabernacle are seen the altar of holocausts and, to the left, the bronze laver which served as a wash basin for the priests.

The Tabernacle proper included the Holy of Holies and the Holy Place. The Holy of Holies contained the Ark of the Covenant. The Holy Place contained the altar of incense (pictured on the left), the table of showbread (shown below) and the seven-branched candlestick.

men among the Ancients of Israel, who were to assist him and share his labors.

Twelve Spies

When the Israelites came to the borders of the Promised Land, Moses sent out twelve men to explore the country. They returned after forty days and told them of the "land flowing with milk and honey." They brought back some of the fruits they had gathered to show its fertility. Most of these spies tried their best to discourage the Israelites from entering the land by telling them its people were mighty giants.

Israelites Punished

Joshua and Caleb were the two most trustworthy spies and tried to persuade the people to enter the country. But the people began complaining again and so God punished them by condemning them to roam the desert for forty years. Not one over 21 years of age who had left Egypt would be allowed to enter the Promised Land.

Revolt of Korah

After having been defeated by the Canaanites, 250 leaders of the nation, led by Korah, a Levite, and Dathan and Abiram of the tribe of Reuben, rebelled against Moses and Aaron. These three men, together with their families and possessions, were punished by God. The ground on which they stood opened up and swallowed Dathan and Abiram; and Korah and his men were consumed by a fire sent by God. A cover was then made and placed over the altar to remind the people that no layman should approach the altar to offer incense to the Lord.

Aaron's Rod

To prove that Aaron was the true High Priest, God ordered Moses to take a staff from each of the twelve tribes and write the name of the chief on it. These Moses laid before the Lord in the tent of the commandments. The next morning,

Aaron's rod was found to bear both blossoms and fruit, while the other rods remained unchanged. After this, the people never doubted the right of Aaron's family to the High Priesthood.

Sin of Moses and Aaron

During the years the Israelites roamed the desert, they came to a place called Kadesh. Here they settled and here it was that Miriam, the sister of Moses and Aaron, died and was buried.

Since there was no water in this place, the people held a council against Moses and Aaron. They complained that it would have been better if they had died with their kinsmen before coming to Kadesh, where there was neither water nor fruit. So Moses and Aaron prayed to God.

The Lord heard their prayer and told Moses to strike the rock and it would yield water for the people and their livestock. But Moses and Aaron showed a lack of confidence in God while carrying out this order; for Moses struck the rock twice, saying to the people: "Are we to bring forth water for you out of this rock?" Because of their doubt, God punished Moses and Aaron by not allowing them to lead His people into the Promised Land. These are the waters of Meribah, where the Israelites contended against the Lord and He revealed His sanctity to them.

Death of Aaron

They then journeyed to Mount Hor, where God told Moses that Aaron was about to die and that his son Eleazar was to be the next High Priest. So Moses invested Eleazar with Aaron's robes, and there on the mountaintop Aaron died.

Bronze Serpent

Since the king of Edom would not allow the Israelites to pass through his territory, the people again complained at the long journey they had to take. They also told Moses that they were tired of eating the manna. To punish them, God sent poisonous serpents out of the sand, which killed great numbers of the people who were bitten by them. Moses begged God to take away the serpents. The Lord told Moses to make a serpent out of bronze and set it up on a pole; anyone who looked at it with faith would be cured. This bronze serpent is a type of our Lord on the Cross.

Balaam

As the Israelites continued on their journey, they met several nations which they defeated by the power of God. When Balak, king of Moab, saw how these people had overcome so many nations, he sent Balaam, a false prophet, to put a curse on the Israelites. But Balaam was unable to do this because the spirit of God prevented him and he cried out: "How can I curse that which God does not curse? How beautiful are your tents, O Israel! A star shall come forth from Jacob, and a staff shall rise out of Israel and shall strike the chiefs of Moab."

Since Balaam had no power to curse the Israelites, he persuaded both the Moabites and the Midianites to corrupt the people by bad example and by leading them into adoring the idol Baal. God ordered Moses to have those who had worshiped the idol Baal publicly executed. This was carried out by the Judges.

Death of Moses

After these Israelites had been killed, God ordered Moses and Eleazar, the High Priest, to number the people again, which they did. Moses knew that he was soon to die, so he reminded the people of all God had done for them. Then he read the chief portions of the law, teaching them the Great Commandment: "You shall love the Lord, your God, with all your heart, and with all your soul, and with all your strength."

After this, Moses went up to Mount Nebo, from where he saw the Promised Land. There, in the land of Moab, Moses died at the age of 120 years, and was buried in a ravine in that land, though to this day no one knows the place of his burial.

JOSHUA

Joshua belonged to the tribe of Reuben. Out of all those who had left Egypt, Joshua and Caleb were the only ones over 21 years old allowed to enter the Promised Land. God told Joshua that he was to lead the people across the Jordan River into the land which He had promised to Abraham.

Two Spies

Joshua sent two spies into Jericho to inspect the land. These men were hid in the home of a woman named **Rahab**, who protected them from the king's men. After spending three days in the hills, the men returned to Joshua. They told him that the people of that country were afraid of the Israelites, so there would be no difficulty in taking over the land.

The Israelites march around Jericho with the ark.

Crossing the Jordan

Joshua gave the command for the people to cross the Jordan. The priests he told to carry the Ark of the Covenant and go ahead of the people. When they reached the river's edge, the waters backed up on either side, forming a dry passage for all to pass through. Seven nations inhabited that country. The power of the Lord was with Joshua and he conquered all these nations.

Taking of Jericho

The Israelites encamped at Gilgal after crossing the Jordan. There they celebrated the Passover. From then on, no manna was supplied and they ate the produce of the land.

Joshua commanded the people to march around the city, which lay in a state of siege. This they did for six days. On the seventh day, they marched around seven times with the priests blowing the trumpets. At the sound of the trumpets, the people all shouted and the walls of the city collapsed.

Taking of Ai

The people thought this city could be taken easily. So they sent only three thousand men against it, but they were badly defeated. Then God told Joshua that one of their number had sinned. They drew lots and the lot fell upon **Achan** of the tribe of Judah. He confessed that he had disobeyed and kept some of the spoils of Jericho. For this he was stoned to death. After that, the Israelites took Ai by stratagem, killing all its inhabitants.

Joshua then built an altar to the Lord and the law was read to all the people. The people swore to keep the commandments of God.

League of Kings

When the kings of the neighboring countries heard that the Israelites had conquered Jericho and Ai, they joined together to attack Joshua, but were defeated.

Then the Gibeonites, a nearby neighbor, sent a delegation to Joshua at Gilgal. They deceived him, pretending they were from a far-off country, and asked for his protection. Joshua agreed to do this. But when he found out their deception, he condemned them to slavery.

While Joshua was defending these people against the Amorites, he prayed to God and commanded the sun and moon to stand still. God heard his prayer and delivered the Amorites up to him.

Division of Judah

When Joshua had grown old, the Lord told him to divide the land which was still unconquered among the various tribes. The land to the south, bordering Edom and the desert of Zin, was given to the tribe of Judah. Joshua set up the Tabernacle at Shiloh and divided the land as the Lord had commanded.

Cities of Refuge

The tribe of Levi had no land, but 48 cities were assigned to them throughout Israel. This was according to the command God gave to Moses that cities, with their pasture lands and livestock, be given to the priestly tribe.

Then six cities of refuge were set apart, where any man who had killed another accidentally could seek refuge from his enemies. These cities were: Kedesh, Shechem and Hebron, on the west side of the Jordan; and Bezer, Ramoth and Golan, on the east side of that river.

Death of Joshua

This holy patriarch ruled Israel for 25 years. Before his death, he gathered together all the tribes of Israel at Shechem, reminding them of all the Lord had done for them. He made them promise to obey all the commandments of the law, which the people promised to do. Joshua died at the age of 110 years and was buried in the mountain region of Ephraim.

THE JUDGES (ca. 1200-1020 B.C.)

After the death of Joshua, the Israelites were governed by the High Priest. When they obeyed God's commandments, they prospered; but whenever they disobeyed the law, their enemies would oppress them. When they repented, God sent Judges to deliver them.

The major Judges were Ehud, Deborah, Gideon, Jepthah, Eli, and Samuel. Like all the Judges, they were great tribal chiefs who repelled foreign peoples who were invading their country. They did so with God's help and their own ingenuity and prowess. In this way, the Israelites passed from a nomadic and pastoral mode of existence to a sedentary and agricultural civilization.

Othniel, Ehud, and Shamgar

As long as the ancients, who had seen the wonderful things done by God for the Israelites, remained among them, the people kept the Commandments. When that generation died off and another grew up, they began to intermarry with the Canaanites and to worship their idols. God punished them and they were held in slavery by the king of Aram Naharaim. When they repented and called upon the Lord to help them, He sent Othniel, son of Caleb's younger brother, to rescue them. They then had peace for forty years.

But they soon offended God again and He sent the king of Moab to attack and defeat them. They were under this ruler for eighteen years. When they cried out to the Lord, He sent **Ehud,** son of Gera, to lead them in battle against the Moabites. These were conquered by the Israelites and they had peace for eighty years.

Shamgar, son of Anath, saved Israel from the Philistines, killing six hundred of them with a plowshare.

Deborah and Barak

After Ehud died, the Israelites again offended God. So He delivered them over to the Canaanites, who oppressed them for twenty years. Deborah, a holy woman, was judging Israel at that time. When the Israelites repented and called upon the Lord to deliver them, Deborah sent Barak, son of Abinoam, to make war on the Canaanites and deliver Israel from their oppression. The honor of this victory, however, was owed to a woman named **Jael,** who killed **Sisara,** the general of the enemy, while he slept in her tent.

Gideon

Again the Israelites fell into sin and this time God delivered them into the hands of the Midianites for several years. When the people repented and implored the Lord to help them, He sent Gideon, a humble man of the tribe of Manasseh, to deliver them. An angel appeared to Gideon, who told him the Lord was with him and that he was to deliver the people from the Midianites. The Lord worked several miracles for Gideon to help him overcome his fear. When Gideon placed the woolen fleece on the ground, he found it covered with dew the next morning, while the ground all around was dry. Again he placed the fleece on the ground and early the next day he found it perfectly dry, while the ground was covered with dew.

Out of 10,000 men, God told Gideon to take only 300 to defeat the Midianites. He gave them trumpets and torches enclosed in empty jars. At midnight Gideon gave the signal and the Israelites broke the jars filled with flames. Blowing their trumpets and holding the torches, they shouted: "A sword for the Lord and for Gideon!" The Midianites were terrified and began killing one another in their confusion. Gideon ruled Israel for forty years.

Abimelech

Abimelech was one of Gideon's sons. In order to gain power, he murdered all his brothers. He ruled Israel for only three years. Because of the evil he had done, God put enmity between the people of Shechem and Abimelech. As he captured Thebez and was about to set fire to the tower, where all the people had taken refuge, a woman threw a stone down on his head. So that it might not be said that he died by the hand of a woman, he ordered his attendant to stab him.

Tola and Jair

After Abimelech's death, Tola, from the region of Ephraim, rose to save Israel. He ruled Israel for 23 years until his death. He was followed by Jair, who was judge over Israel for 22 years.

Jephthah

The Israelites again turned to worship the false gods of their neighbors. To punish them, God allowed the Ammonites and Philistines to overcome them. At that time there was a man named Jehpthah, the son of Gilead. His brothers cast him out of their home and he became the leader of a band of ruffians.

When the Ammonites attacked Israel, the elders of the people came to ask Jephthah to lead them in battle. When he went out to fight the Ammonites at Mizpah-Gilead, Jephthah promised God that the first person he met coming out of his house after the victory, he would offer as a holocaust. Jephthah was saddened when the first one who came to meet him was his daughter. Jephthah carried out his vow to the Lord.

Then Jephthah defeated the Ephramites and judged Israel for six years.

Samson

God delivered the Israelites into the hands of the Philistines because of their offenses against Him. They were oppressed for forty years. One day, an angel of the Lord appeared to Manoah and his wife and told them they would have a son called Samson, who would deliver Israel. He was to be consecrated to the Lord and his head was not to be shaved. This boy had great strength, for at one time he tore a lion to pieces without any weapon, and at another he killed thirty Philistines. Then he fastened torches to the tails of 300 foxes; he turned them loose in the cornfields and vineyards of the Philistines. After this, his enemies pursued him and took him prisoner through treachery. But Samson broke their bonds and slew 1000 of them with the jaw-bone of an ass. The next time they tried to take him prisoner he escaped by carrying away the gates on his back.

Samson's second wife was named **Delilah**. She soon learned the secret of Samson's strength and told it to the Philistines. Samson's strength came from his hair. One day, while he slept, Delilah cut off his hair. Then the Philistines bound him, put out his eyes, and threw him into prison, where he was made to grind corn.

Samson prayed to God that he would regain his strength. The Lord answered his prayer. While he was in the temple of the Philistines, he took hold of the two middle columns and shook them so violently that the Temple collapsed, killing Samson and all the people in it. Samson had judged Israel for 20 years.

Samson shakes the pillar and destroys the temple of Dagon.

The Philistine Threat

The greatest threat to the Israelites at this time came from the invasions of the Philistines. These were part of the waves of immigrants from the isles of Greece and the coasts of Asia Minor, whom the Egyptians called, "the Peoples of the Sea."

Prevented from conquering Egypt by Rameses III (1175-1144), the Philistines settled along the coastal plain of Canaan, where they established a confederation of city-states. From there, they attempted to seize the whole of the mountain range and they nearly succeeded. Indeed, their own name has been thereafter used to designate the entire land of **Palestine**. They were definitely overcome only at the time of David.

Eli

Eli, a holy man, was judge over Israel for forty years. He had two sons, Hophni and Phinehas, who were both wicked, respecting neither God nor the priestly functions. When Eli heard of their evil deeds, he warned them; but he was not firm with them. God sent His messenger to tell Eli that he and his sons would be punished severely.

When the Philistines waged war against Israel and defeated them, they captured the Ark and brought it to their own temple. Hophni and Phinehas were killed in the battle. When news of all this was brought to Eli, he fell backward from his chair and died.

Now, wherever the Philistines carried the Ark, death and a plague of rats followed in its wake. The Philistines then placed the Ark in a chariot to which they hitched a pair of heifers, placing an offering of gold in the form of the plagues with it. The chariot led by the heifers, without any drivers, immediately went towards Beth-shemesh. By this the Philistines knew that it was the God of Israel who had punished them. The Levites placed the Ark on a large stone and prepared to offer sacrifice. But the people who broke the law by looking upon the Ark when it was uncovered were struck dead.

After this, the inhabitants of Kiriath-jearim brought the Ark to the house of **Abinadab**. His son Eleazar was appointed guardian of the Ark. Here it remained for twenty years and the Israelites repented and turned to the Lord.

Samuel

Samuel was the son of Elkanah and his holy wife, Hannah, who lived at Shiloh. In thanksgiving to God for sending her a child, Hannah dedicated him to the Lord's service from his infancy. After Eli died, Samuel became judge over Israel. He succeeded in getting the people to do away with their false gods. Samuel ordered all the people to gather at Mizpah in order to beg God to forgive them. They poured out water on the ground and fasted, confessing their sins against the Lord.

When Samuel grew old, he appointed his two sons, Joel and Abijah, to be judges over Israel. But these two sons did not follow the good example of their father and accepted bribes. Then the ancients of Israel begged Samuel to give them a king to rule them.

After consulting God, he was told to inform the people of all the demands a king would make of them. In spite of this warning, the people still insisted they wanted a king. The Lord revealed to Samuel that He would send a man from the tribe of Benjamin whom he was to appoint king over the people.

THE REIGN OF SAUL (ca. 1020-1000 B.C.)

Samuel took Saul and anointed him king as the Lord had commanded. When the people came together at Mizpah, Samuel ordered each tribe and each family to draw lots, and the lot fell on Saul of the tribe of Benjamin. When he stood up he was taller than all the people. Then they all shouted: "Long live the king!"

Samuel presents Saul to the people as their King.

Victory over the Ammonites

When Saul heard that the Ammonites had surrounded Jabesh-gilead, he sent messengers to all the people that they were to follow him or they would be cut down. 300,000 Israelites and 70,000 Judahites turned out to support him. The next day, he invaded the enemy's camp and destroyed them.

After that, Samuel called the people together at Gilgal, where he again ordered them to accept Saul as their king. There they sacrificed peace offerings to God.

Withdrawal of Samuel

Before the celebrations ended, Samuel called the people to bear witness to his government in the presence of God. The whole assembly cried out: "You have not cheated or oppressed us. You have not accepted anything from anyone's hand." Then this holy man told them to remain faithful to God, and he warned Saul that if he and the people did not remain faithful to the Lord, He would punish them severely.

Saul's First Sin

Shortly after, the Philistines assembled at Michmash to attack the Israelites. The people were terrified at the sight of so many drawn up against them. Saul waited seven days for Samuel to appear to offer sacrifice. When he was delayed in coming, Saul grew impatient and offered the sacrifice himself, although he was not a priest. Just as he was finished, Samuel arrived and reproved Saul. Then he told him that because he had disobeyed God's command, his kingdom would not endure and would be given to another.

Other Victories

God still made use of Saul to destroy His enemies. Jonathan, Saul's son, together with his armor-bearer, surprised a group of Philistines. The Lord was with him, for the men thought they had been betrayed and turned on one another. In the confusion, the Israelites, with Saul at their head, rushed in and completely defeated their enemies. Saul fought bravely and overcame many of the surrounding nations.

Saul's Second Sin

Samuel told Saul that God wanted him to march against the Amalekites and overcome them. But Saul again disobeyed the Lord. For though he defeated the people, he did not destroy the best of the livestock.

Samuel rebuked Saul, telling him that he had displeased the Lord. Saul tried to excuse his disobedience by saying he had kept the spoils to offer in sacrifice to God. Samuel said to Saul: "Obedience is better than sacrifice. Therefore God has rejected you and chosen another." Samuel then had Agag put to death.

Election of David

After this, God sent Samuel to Jesse in Bethlehem; for He had chosen one of his sons to be king in place of Saul. Samuel took a heifer with him to offer sacrifice, as the Lord commanded. When they all gathered for the banquet, Jesse presented his sons to Samuel. But the Lord told Samuel that none of these was the one He had chosen. At last, the youngest son was brought in from the fields. At the Lord's order, Samuel anointed David before all his brothers. From then on the Spirit of the Lord rested upon David.

On the contrary, an evil spirit entered into Saul. His servants told him that they knew of a young man in Bethlehem who was a fine harpist and who could soothe his troubled spirit. So David was brought to Saul. His playing so pleased Saul that he made him his armor-bearer.

David and Goliath

Then the Philistines decided to attack Israel. The two armies were encamped opposite each other. They had among their number a giant, named Goliath, who defied the Israelites and dared one of them to engage in combat with him.

Meantime, Jesse sent David to the camp to bring provisions to his brothers who were fighting in Saul's army. David assured Saul he would deliver Israel from the insults of the giant Philistine.

Armed with only his shepherd's staff and sling, David took five stones from the brook. He put his entire trust in the

David prepares his sling to fell Goliath.

power of God. Then putting a stone in his sling, he hurled it at Goliath. The stone was buried in the giant's brain and he fell to the ground. Then David cut off Goliath's head with his own sword. When the Philistines saw that their giant was dead, they dispersed and Israel won an easy victory.

Jealousy of Saul

As David was returning, the women came out to greet him, dancing and singing songs of triumph: "Saul has slain his thousands, and David his tens of thousands." This made Saul very angry, and he became jealous of David and sought to kill him. David took refuge with Ahimelech, the high priest, at Nob. When Saul heard this, he killed all the people of Nob, including 85 priests.

David Spares Saul

On two different occasions after this, Saul was in David's power, but his life was spared each time. The first time, Saul entered the cave where David and his men were hiding. David cut off the hem of the king's robe and allowed him to go away. The next time he entered Saul's tent at night, while the guards were asleep, and took his goblet and lance.

When David showed him these things, Saul saw that God was truly with David and had remorse for his deeds. In the meantime Samuel died. All Israel mourned him and he was buried in Ramah.

Witch of Endor

Because of Saul's disobedience and lack of faith, God allowed the Philistines to wage war against him. In his despair, Saul consulted a witch, or medium, about the outcome of the struggle. Samuel's ghost appeared and told Saul that the next day he and his sons would be killed and Israel delivered into the hands of the enemy.

Saul's Death

The next day it happened as Samuel had predicted. The Israelites fled before the advancing Philistines and Saul and his sons were wounded. Saul asked his armor-bearer to slay him with the sword, but the man refused and Saul fell upon his own sword. Then the armor-bearer, seeing that Saul and his sons were dead, took his own life. When the news of the death of Saul and his sons reached David, he and all his men mourned and fasted for Saul and Jonathan, and all those Israelites who had fallen by the sword.

THE REIGN OF DAVID (ca. 1000-962 B.C.)

David Anointed King

After Saul's death, David asked the Lord whether he should go to one of the cities of Judah. God told him to go to Hebron. So David went there with his two wives, taking his men and their families with him. There he was anointed king by the Judahites.

Ishbaal

Abner, Saul's general, placed Saul's son, Ishbaal, on the throne of Israel. Ishbaal reigned over Israel for two years. David ruled as king of the Judahites for seven years.

The two sides met at Gibeon. Abner and the servants of Ishbaal, and Joab with David's servants, took up arms. After a fierce battle, Israel was defeated. Asahel, the brother of Joab, pursued Abner, but was killed by Abner.

Abner Killed

A long war was carried on between the Judahites and the Israelites. During this time, Ishbaal treated Abner unjustly, so Abner sent messengers to David for a reconciliation. David agreed, on condition that Saul's daughter Michal whom he had married, be brought to him. Peace was made between David and Abner.

When Joab heard this, he was angry and stabbed Abner at Hebron in revenge for his brother's death. David and the people mourned the death of Abner and David fasted all day.

Ishbaal's Death

While Ishbaal was asleep, two of his officers killed him and cut off his head, which they brought to David. Instead of the reward they expected to receive, David had them put to death for the terrible crime they had committed.

All the tribes of Israel then came to David in Hebron. They reminded him of what the Lord had said to him: "You shall shepherd My people Israel." So David made an agreement with them before the Lord and was anointed king of Israel. David reigned for forty years: seven years over Judah and 33 years over both Israel and Judah.

Taking of Zion

Then King David and his men marched on Jerusalem. The people of this city relied on the strong walls of the city to protect them. But David took over the city and made it his capital.

After consulting the Lord, David attacked the Philistines, who had come out against him. God was with him and he defeated them.

David sings and dances while taking the Ark to Jerusalem.

The Ark

David and all the people went to Baala in Judah to bring the Ark of the Lord to Jerusalem. On the journey, Uzzah put out his hand to steady the Ark which seemed about to fall. He was struck dead for breaking the law. King David danced for joy before the Ark of the Lord and all the people joined in the festivities for this great occasion. The Ark was placed in the tent David had set up for it.

Victories of David

Wherever David undertook a battle, the Lord made him victorious. First he defeated the Philistines and took all their possessions. His next battle was with the king of Zobah. He subdued the power of the Ammonites, the Moabites and the Arameans. The kingdom of David now extended from the Euphrates River to the Mediterranean Sea, and from Phoenicia to the Arabian Sea.

The Sin of David

While David was walking on the roof of his palace, he saw a beautiful woman. Her name was Bathsheba and she was the wife of Uriah, Joab's armor-bearer. In order to obtain this woman for his wife, David ordered Joab to place Uriah where the fighting was heaviest. This order was carried out and Uriah was killed in battle.

Punishment of David

The Lord God was angry with David. After a year had passed, He sent the prophet **Nathan** to remind David of his sin and to tell him that the son born to Bathsheba would die. Nathan also told David that the Lord would send evil upon his house.

This came about, for David's son Absalom killed his half-brother Ammon and fled the country. David later pardoned Absalom and he returned.

It was not long after that Absalom plotted to divide the kingdom. He won over many of the Israelites to his side and declared himself king of Israel. David, with his officers and his household, left the palace and fled from the city. Then Absalom entered Jerusalem with the Israelites and committed the most frightful sins, even in public. But David gathered his troops about him and defeated Absalom, whom Joab killed as he hung by his hair from a terebinth tree.

New Sin of David

After the death of Absalom, David returned in triumph to Jerusalem.

Then David ordered Joab and his men to take a census of all the people of Israel and Judah. This he did out of pride. To punish him, God sent a plague which killed 70,000 of the people.

When David saw this, he said to the Lord: "I am the one who has sinned and done wrong. These are but sheep; what have they done? Let your hand fall upon me and my family." Then David built an altar to the Lord and offered sacrifice of atonement.

Anointing of Solomon

As David was advanced in age, he kept his vow to Bathsheba that their son Solomon would succeed him on the throne. So Zadok the priest and Nathan the prophet anointed Solomon king. They blew the trumpet and all the people shouted: "Long live King Solomon!"

Death of David

As the time of David's death drew near, he gave Solomon his last instructions. He told him always to walk in the ways of God, observing all His laws and decrees as written in the law of Moses.

David died at the age of 77 years and was buried in the City of David. He left a glorious memory in the minds of his people. He is considered a noble king, an inspired prophet and a sublime poet. Several works were written by him, including the **Psalms**.

THE REIGN OF SOLOMON (ca. 962-922 B.C.)

This king was famous for his exceptional wisdom and great wealth. His reign began with a revolt, for his brother Adonijah, together with Joab and the priest Abiathar, tried to dethrone Solomon, but he had them executed.

Alliance with Egypt

With his kingdom solidly established, Solomon married Pharaoh's daughter and thus formed an alliance with Egypt.

Solomon had a dream in which the Lord appeared to him, telling him to ask whatever he wished. Solomon, realizing the great number of people he had to govern, humbly asked God to give him the gift of wisdom, to be able to judge the people rightly and to discern between good and evil. God was pleased with this request, and gave Solomon great wealth and glory as well.

The Lord speaks to Solomon in a dream.

Judgment of Solomon

An occasion soon arose to show the wisdom God had bestowed on him. Two women stood before the king with a child. Each one claimed it as her own. Solomon ordered the child to be cut in two and half given to each of the women. The woman whose child it was told him to give the infant to the other woman rather than have it killed. Solomon knew at once that this was the real mother and gave the child to her. All the people were in admiration of the king for the wisdom God had given him.

Solomon's Glory

Solomon ruled over the vast territory of Judah and Israel and all the people lived in peace and security. He had fleets which traded with other countries, bringing back their costly products to add to the splendor of his kingdom.

The great work of Solomon's reign, however, was the building of the Temple of Jerusalem in honor of the Lord, as God had predicted to David. Hiram, king of Tyre, contributed the cedar and fir trees for this building. The temple was built of stone, which was cut and prepared at the quarry. Thus, no hammer, axe or iron tool was heard in the temple during its construction.

Many thousands of men were employed to accomplish this work, including Israelites, Egyptians and Syrians. It took seven years to build it. When it was completed, Solomon called together all the chief men at Jerusalem. All walked in procession, with the priests carrying the Ark of the Lord and all the sacred vessels.

When the priests had deposited the Ark in its place, a cloud filled the temple and the glory of the Lord filled the place. Then King Solomon made a solemn prayer of petition to God, after which sacrifices were offered.

As well as the temple, Solomon built a palace for himself at Jerusalem and one for his queen. The soldiers on guard carried arms of gold. In addition, he built several new towns and fortified those that were defenseless.

God promised Solomon that as long as he kept all His laws and decrees, some one of his descendants would always sit on the throne of Israel. However, if he or his descendants failed to keep the commandments and statutes, Israel would be cut off from the land and the temple reduced to ruins. Men would know that it was because Israel forsook the Lord and turned to worship false gods that the Lord brought all this evil upon them.

Queen of Sheba

This queen heard of Solomon's great wisdom and glory. She traveled a long distance from Arabia and brought many priceless gifts to Solomon. But most of all, she wanted to question him on many matters. His answers and explanations so astonished her that she exclaimed in admiration of his wisdom, saying: "Blessed be the Lord, your God, Who has delighted in you and placed you on the throne of Israel. In His enduring love for Israel, the Lord has made you king to maintain justice and righteousness."

Sins of Solomon

Besides the daughter of Pharaoh, Solomon intermarried with women of nations forbidden by God. These served idols and soon he turned to false gods. God told him that since he had not kept His covenant and statutes the kingdom would be taken away from his descendants. God told him that only one tribe would be left to his son because of the promise the Lord made to David.

After this, God sent several adversaries against Solomon. Then the prophet **Ahijah** told Jeroboam, one of Solomon's servants who had rebelled against him, that he would reign over ten of the tribes of Israel. Solomon reigned in Jerusalem over all Israel for forty years. Solomon died and was buried in the City of David.

THE DIVISION OF THE TRIBES (922 B.C.)

Solomon's son, **Rehoboam**, succeeded him and was anointed at Shechem. The elders, under the leadership of

Jeroboam, asked the young king to lessen their oppressive burdens laid upon them by Solomon. But he would not listen to them and took the advice of the younger men around him and increased the burdens of the people.

Then ten of the tribes placed themselves under **Jeroboam** as their king. So the kingdom of Israel divided: the ten tribes formed the new kingdom of Israel, while the tribes of Judah and Benjamin formed the new kingdom of Judah, and were governed by **Rehoboam.**

THE KINGDOM OF ISRAEL (922-722 B.C.)

Jeroboam had two golden calves made and encouraged the people to worship these instead of going to Jerusalem to worship in the temple. He did this to prevent them from returning to King Rehoboam.

From Jeroboam to Ahab (922-850 B.C.)

Although prophets came to warn Jeroboam that God would punish him for his wickedness, he continued in his sinful life, consecrating priests from among the common people who were not of the house of Aaron. The prophet Ahijah told him that God was angry with him, and because he worshiped idols evil would be brought upon him, for all the males in his line would be completely destroyed. Jeroboam ruled for 22 years. His entire family was wiped out.

Jeroboam's son, Nadab, succeeded his father, but only reigned over Israel for two years. He was just as wicked as his father. **Baasha**, son of Ahijah, of the tribe of Issachar, plotted against Nadab and killed him. When the Lord sent the prophet Jehu to warn Baasha that he would come to the same end as Jeroboam and his house, he killed Jehu. Baasha reigned in Israel for 24 years.

His son **Elah** succeeded him, ruling for only two years. Elah's servant, Zimri, plotted against him and killed him and his whole household, as the Lord had prophesied. Zimri reigned only seven days.

Omri became king of Israel and ruled for twelve years. He had been general of the army and was chosen by the army to be king. His life, too, was sinful. When he died he was buried in Samaria.

Ahab was Omri's son and reigned over Israel in Samaria for 22 years. This king was more evil than any of his predecessors. He married a very wicked woman named **Jezebel**, and worshiped the god Baal, building an altar in Samaria.

The prophet **Elijah** predicted the drought, which lasted for three years because of the sins of Ahab.

During this period Elijah was instructed by God to go to Zarephath, where a certain widow would take care of his needs. Upon asking her to prepare him some food, the widow told him there was just a little left to make a meal for her son and herself. But Elijah encouraged her to do as he asked, telling her the Lord would provide for her. So she prepared food for Elijah and was able to provide for her son and herself, as Elijah had predicted.

Elijah then worked a great miracle before the people by calling on God to send fire from heaven to consume the

In answer to Elijah's prayer fire consumes the holocaust.

holocaust. The false prophets of Baal called on their god, but of course nothing happened. Then the people seized the prophets of Baal and put them to death.

Ahab wanted a vineyard belonging to a man named **Naboth**, but Naboth refused to give up his heritage. By means of lies, Jezebel succeeded in having Naboth discredited before the Elders, who put him to death. Ahab then took possession of Naboth's vineyard.

From Ahaziah to Jeroboam II (849-740 B.C.)

Ahab died in battle and was succeeded by his son, **Ahaziah**, who was as evil as his father and mother. He reigned only two years.

Joram was the brother of Ahaziah and succeeded him as king, since Ahaziah had no son. He was equally as bad as his brother. He and his remaining brothers were put to death by Jehu, who had been chosen by God to succeed to the throne of Israel. Jezebel also was killed, and her corpse eaten by dogs in Naboth's vineyard, as the Lord had said.

Jehu went to Samaria, where he killed the remaining members of Ahab's line. This fulfilled the prophecy God had spoken through Elijah. Then Jehu called all the worshipers of Baal to come to the temple. While they were offering sacrifice to Baal he had them all killed. Jehu did not observe the law of God, for he forbade the people to go to Jerusalem. Therefore God allowed the king of Syria to ravage his country. Jehu ruled over Israel in Samaria for 28 years.

Joash remained faithful as long as the prophet **Elisha** lived. He won many victories over the Syrians. He also defeated the king of Judah. Then he plundered the temple and the palace of their gold and silver, bringing the spoils as well as hostages back to Samaria. He died a year later and was buried in that country.

Jeroboam II was the son of Joash and reigned 41 years in Israel. He was just as wicked as Jeroboam I. The Lord took pity on Israel and used this wicked king to restore her territory, as He had prophesied through the prophet Jonah.

The Fall of Samaria (746-722 B.C.)

Zechariah succeeded his father and ruled Israel for only six months. He followed the bad example of his father and was put to death by **Shallum**, who only ruled one month. Shallum was defeated and killed by **Menahem**, son of Gadi.

Menahem also followed the evil example of Jeroboam. He tried to strengthen his power by cruel tyranny. The king of Assyria attacked him, but he bought peace by paying a thousand talents of silver, which he obtained from the rich. Menahem did not live long after this and was succeeded by his son **Pekahiah**, who reigned only two years. Pekahiah's adjutant, Pekah, conspired against him and put him to death.

During the reign of **Pekah**, Judah abandoned the God of their fathers and the Lord delivered them into the hands of Pekah, who won a complete victory over Ahaz, king of Judah. But the king of Assyria attacked and destroyed parts of Israel and deported the inhabitants to his own country. Pekah was killed by Hoshea, after a reign of twenty years.

Hoshea ruled Israel only nine years, and he too led an evil life. Because the Israelites had sinned against the Lord, He sent Shalmaneser V, king of Assyria, to attack Israel. During the first attack, Hoshea became vassal to Shalmaneser and paid tribute to him. When Hoshea was found guilty of conspiracy and of refusing to pay the tribute, he was taken prisoner by Shalmaneser. Then this king attacked Israel, laying siege to Samaria for three years.

During the siege, Shalmaneser V died and his son Sargon II came to power. His army finally took possession of Samaria and he carried away to Babylonia some 28,000 of the elite inhabitants of the Northern Kingdom. At the same time, he resettled the conquered territory with people from Babylonia and Syria. These new people intermingled with the peasant classes left in Israel and their descendants became known as the Samaritans.

THE KINGDOM OF JUDAH (922-586 B.C.)

Although many of the kings of Judah were evil, there were some who were faithful and governed the people with justice. Unlike Israel, the kingdom of Judah retained the worship of the true God and had the true order of the priesthood.

From Rehoboam to Jehoshaphat (922-849 B.C.)

Rehoboam, the son of Solomon, reigned in Jerusalem for 17 years. In the beginning of his reign the people remained faithful to God. However, as soon as they thought they were secure, they turned to the worship of idols and followed the customs of their pagan nations. The Lord punished them by permitting Shishak, the king of Egypt, to attack Jerusalem. He plundered the city, even to taking the temple treasures.

Abijam waged war against Jeroboam, king of Israel. Although an ambush was laid by Israel to attack Judah from behind, the people of Judah cried out to the Lord for help. God heard their prayer and Jeroboam and his army were defeated. But Abijam was unfaithful to God and committed the same sins as his father. He reigned only three years.

Asa, son of Abijam, came to the throne as a child. He was a good and pious king like David, in spite of his wicked grandmother, who tried to spread idolatry. Asa had her deposed when he was old enough to govern. Then he destroyed the heathen altars and broke the idols in pieces. Under Asa's rule, the people returned to God and there was peace in the kingdom for ten years.

As long as he relied on the Lord, Asa won many victories. But during the last years of his reign, he put his trust in another king instead of trusting in the Lord. When God sent the prophet Hannai to reproach him, he became angry and put the prophet in prison. Asa was struck with a disease, but even then he did not seek the help of God. He died in the forty-first year of his reign.

Jehoshaphat, son of Asa, came to the throne at the age of 35. He was a good king and followed the laws of God. He sent the priests, Elishama and Jehoram, together with the Levites, to visit the cities of Judah and teach the people. God rewarded him for his fidelity and he became very powerful so that all his enemies feared him.

Jehoshaphat committed the grave error of marrying his son to the daughter of Ahab, king of Israel, thus making an alliance with Ahab. Although warned by the prophet Micaiah, the two kings engaged in battle against the king of Aram. When Jehoshaphat was about to be slain, he cried out to the Lord, Who came to his aid and he was spared. Jehoshaphat repented and brought the people back to God. He also appointed judges to settle their disputes.

When Jehoshaphat was informed that the Moabites were preparing to attack him, he ordered a fast in all of Judah and prayed fervently to the Lord. God sent the prophet Jahaziah to tell the king and the people that He was with them. After adoring God, they engaged in battle against the Moabites and won a great victory. Jehoshaphat reigned 25 years in Jerusalem.

From Jehoram to Ahaz (849-715 B.C.)

Jehoram, Jehoshaphat's son, did not lead a virtuous life like his father. He followed the bad advice of his wife, a daughter of Ahab, king of Israel, and led the people into idolatry. God sent the prophet Elijah to tell him that he and his family would be stricken by a plague because he had sinned against the Lord.

The Philistines and the Arabs invaded Judah and took all his wealth. He himself was afflicted with a horrible disease and died in severe pain after a reign of eight years. He was refused royal burial.

Ahaziah, the youngest son of Jehoram, then came to the throne. He followed the evil ways of his father and reigned only one year in Jerusalem.

His mother, Athaliah, ordered all the king's relatives put to death, but one son, Joash, escaped. He was rescued by his father's sister, who was the wife of the high-priest Jehoiada, and was brought up by him in secret. Meanwhile, Athaliah had idols set up throughout the country.

When Joash grew up, he was brought from hiding and anointed king by Jehoiada. Athaliah was executed by order of the high priest.

Joash remained faithful to the Lord as long as Jehoiada lived. He had the temple restored and offered holocausts to the Lord.

When the holy priest died, King Joash became wicked and turned to worshiping idols. When he was accused of his sins by the prophet Zechariah, son of Jehoiada, the king had him stoned to death.

The Lord punished Judah by sending the Arameans against them. Joash was defeated, and murdered by his own servants, after a reign of forty years. He, too, was denied royal burial.

Amaziah, the son of Joash, succeeded him on the throne of Judah and reigned for 29 years. While he himself served the Lord, he still permitted the people to keep their shrines and to offer sacrifice to idols.

He conquered and slew the Edomites and was reproved for this by the king of Israel. Then the Israelites advanced on Judah and destroyed Jerusalem, stripping the Lord's temple of all the sacred vessels. Amaziah was assassinated while escaping from Jerusalem.

Azariah was only sixteen years old when he succeeded his father to the throne, and he ruled for 52 years. As long as the prophet **Zechariah** lived, Azariah remained faithful to the

Lord. With God's help, he defeated the neighboring nations and made many improvements in the country.

After he became powerful, he also became proud and offended God. He burned incense in the temple and was rebuked for this sin by the priest. For this grievous offense the Lord afflicted him with leprosy.

Jotham, son of Azariah, came to the throne and reigned in Jerusalem for sixteen years. He was a virtuous king and God was with him in all his undertakings. Jotham built the Upper Gate of the Temple. His son Ahaz succeeded him as king of Judah.

Ahaz also ruled for sixteen years, but, unlike his father, was a very wicked king. He worshiped idols, and sacrificed his own son by fire, according to the practice of his pagan neighbors. He refused to listen to the prophet Isaiah.

Ahaz suffered many defeats and called upon the king of Assyria to help him. He plundered the house of the Lord to pay tribute to this king. After he had offered sacrifice to all the abominable gods to obtain their help, he suffered even worse disasters. Finally, in his anger, he broke the sacred vessels in pieces. When he died he was deprived of royal burial because of his evil life.

Hezekiah (715-687 B.C.) and the Siege of Jerusalem (701 B.C.)

Hezekiah, son of Ahaz, became king and ruled for 29 years. He was the opposite of his father and served the Lord faithfully. In the first month of his reign, he opened the doors of the temple and had it cleansed and restored to its former splendor. Then he called the Levites and the princes of the people together, and sacrifices and offerings of thanksgiving were made to God. The Passover was celebrated by all the people gathered together, and many liturgical reforms were made.

Hezekiah did all to fulfill the will of God and the Lord stood by him. Judah was threatened by Sennacherib, king of Assyria, who tried to turn the people against their king. But

Hezekiah and the prophet Isaiah prayed and called on the Lord to help them. God sent an angel through the Assyrian camp and 185,000 men were destroyed in one night. Sennacherib returned to his own country.

Hezekiah fell seriously ill and was told by Isaiah to prepare for death. But Hezekiah begged the Lord to heal him and spare his life. The Lord granted his prayer and added fifteen years more to his life. When he died all of Judah honored him.

Manasseh, Amon and Josiah 687-609 B.C.

Manasseh, son of Hezekiah, came to the throne and was as wicked as his father was virtuous. He worshiped idols and even built altars to Baal in the Lord's temple. Indeed, there was no evil that this king did not perform, for he shed much innocent blood in Jerusalem, and had his own son immolated by fire.

God permitted the king of Assyria to attack Judah, and Manasseh was bound in chains and brought to Babylon. Then Manasseh repented of his evil deeds and humbled himself before the Lord, begging His forgiveness. God heard his prayer and he was returned to his kingdom in Jerusalem.

Amon, the son of Manasseh, became king of Judah and reigned only two years. He was very wicked, offering to idols, as his father had done. He was put to death by his own servants, and his son, Josiah, came to rule in his place.

Josiah was only eight years old when he became king, and reigned 31 years. While he was still young, he began to serve the God of David, his forefather, and to cleanse all of Judah from the stain of idolatry.

The temple was restored. During this work, the priest Hilkiah found the book of the law which had been given by the Lord through Moses. When the book was brought to the king, he gathered the priests, the prophets and all the people in the temple and had the law read to them.

Josiah was killed in a battle against Neco, king of Egypt, and all Judah mourned his loss.

The End of Judah 609-586 B.C.

Jehoahaz, son of Josiah, was proclaimed king by the people. He was not like his father and led a very wicked life. He only reigned for three months, being taken prisoner by the king of Egypt and died in captivity.

Jehoiakim was the brother of Jehoahaz and was placed on the throne by the king of Egypt. He reigned eleven years in Jerusalem and was as evil as his brother. During his reign, the Lord carried out His threat against Judah because of the sins of Manasseh in shedding innocent blood.

After his death, he was succeeded by his son Jehoiachin, who reigned only three months before Nebuchadnezzar captured Jerusalem in 597 B.C. after a three-month siege. The foreign ruler pillaged the Temple and palace, and took ten thousand of the prominent men, princes, warriors, priests and craftsmen and transplanted them to Babylonia together with Jehoiachin. In his place, he enthroned Zedekiah, his uncle.

Zedekiah ruled eleven years in Jerusalem. He also was evil and rejected the word of God spoken to him by the prophet Jeremiah. The priests and the people committed atrocious crimes and defiled the Temple of the Lord.

THE BABYLONIAN CAPTIVITY (586-538 B.C.)

Fall of Jerusalem

Again and again God sent His prophets to warn the people, for He wished to spare them. But the people paid no attention to these messengers and scoffed at them. In the end they incurred the punishment the prophets had predicted.

In 588 Zedekiah, counting on help from Hophra, king of Egypt, and refusing to listen to the prophet Jeremiah, revolted against Assyria. In retaliation, Nebuchadnezzar again besieged Jerusalem and finally captured it in 586. The city was completely demolished, the Temple and all public build-ings were burned, and the country was laid waste. The prophet Jeremiah remained in Jerusalem after its destruction, but was later exiled to Egypt.

Fate of the Exiles

Thousands of Judeans were again deported to Babylonia, making a total of some fifty thousand that Nebuchadnezzar had carried away in two deportations. Some of the people fared well. They were allowed to live their normal lives, according to their own laws. Many, however, were reduced to slavery and suffered under the yoke of their oppressors.

Little by little, the exiles became accustomed to their new life. They adopted the names, the calendar and the writings of the Babylonians. They even forgot the Hebrew language and began to speak Aramaic which, in time, became the common language of the Chosen People.

The Prophet Ezekiel

The prophet Ezekiel who had been taken into exile in 597, worked hard to encourage and comfort his suffering

Ezekiel prophesies over the dried bones of Israel.

people. He told them: (1) The Lord would save them when they returned to Him. (2) He would purify them with water and sanctify them with the gifts of the Spirit. (3) He would give them a faithful shepherd, the new David. (4) He would dwell in the new Temple in order to renew His friendship with them. (5) In the New Covenant each individual would suffer for his sins. (6) In the New Kingdom founded by the Messiah all nations would enter.

The Prophet Daniel

The prophet Daniel also spoke to the Jews who lived near the canals of Babylon. He repeated to them that God sought their conversion or repentance by means of the suffering they were undergoing.

The Prophet Called "Second Isaiah"

As the years passed, the important personages in exile in Babylon died. Many exiles began to doubt the promises of a return to Jerusalem. Then a distant disciple of the prophet Isaiah wrote the "Book of Consolation of Israel," found in chapters 40—55 of the Book of Isaiah. He announced to the Jews that they would soon be liberated. For this purpose God would make use of Cyrus, king of the Persians.

The prophet saw Israel, servant of Yahweh, in painful exile, where the Lord was to purify it of its sins and save it through suffering. Then he thought of another Servant—the Redeemer, Who would save the world by suffering.

The Book of Consolation helped to guide the Messianic hope of the poor. It indicated that the Messiah was to be sought not among the powerful of the world but among the poor, those who lived according to the spirit of the prophets.

THE RETURN AND RESTORATION (538-515 B.C.)
The Return

In 538 Cyrus carried out Second Isaiah's prophecy and captured Babylon without waging a battle. He overran the Babylonian Empire, and reversed the policy of mass deportations by allowing the captives, including the Jews, to return to their lands and build their temples.

Over 40,000 Jews returned under the leadership of Zerubbabel and Jeshua, although some elected to remain in Babylon, continuing to practice their religion as best they could.

The Restoration

A new community was formed out of a combination of the Judean peasants who had remained in Palestine and kept up their religion and the more intelligent of the religious devotees who had returned from exile where they had cherished the laws of the past and framed codes for the future.

In 538-515 the Jewish colony which occupied but a small territory about Jerusalem under Zerubbabel began to construct the Temple. The people of Samaria tried to keep the

The Israelites begin to rebuild the Temple.

Jews from carrying out their work of building. They sent a letter to the king advising him to stop the city walls from being erected, giving as the reason that the people would rebel once their city was rebuilt. So the king gave an order to stop the building.

Then the prophets **Haggai** and **Zechariah** began to prophesy in the name of the Lord and to encourage the people to proceed with the construction work. When all was completed, the Temple was dedicated and sacrifices were offered to God, as prescribed in the book of Moses.

Ezra and Nehemiah

The ancient laws and customs were restored under the leadership of two dedicated men.

About 445, **Nehemiah** a court official of Artaxerxes I, secured the governorship of Judah and rebuilt the walls of the Holy City; he reorganized the Jewish community as distinct from the Samaritans. In 389 **Ezra** arrived in Jerusalem and established the observance of the Mosaic Law (Neh 8) and the renewal of the Covenant.

THE PROPHETS

The Role of the Prophets

The prophetic books of the Bible, together with the oral preaching of the prophets, were the result of the institution of prophetism, in which a succession of Israelites chosen by God and appointed by Him to be prophets, received communications from Him and transmitted them to the people in His name.

The prophets were spokesmen of God, intermediaries between Him and His people. The communications they received from God came through visions, dreams, and ecstasies and were transmitted to the people through sermons, writings, and symbolic actions.

The office of prophet was due to a direct call from God. It was not the result of heredity, just as it was not a permanent gift but a transient one, subject entirely to the divine will. The prophets preserved and developed revealed religion, denounced idolatry, defended the moral law, gave counsel in political matters, and often also in matters of private life. At times miracles confirmed their preaching, and their predictions of the future intensified the expectation of the Messiah and of His kingdom.

The literary form of prophecy uses warning and threat besides exhortation and promise to declare in God's name events of the near and distant future. Kind and persuasive tones pervade the promises of reward and even the threats of punishment.

Types of Prophets

There were four major "writing prophets" and twelve minor ones and Baruch, who was a disciple of Jeremiah. They are called major and minor prophets because of the length of their writings and not because of any distinction among them.

The four major prophets are: Isaiah, Jeremiah, Ezekiel and Daniel.

The twelve minor prophets are: Hosea, Joel, Amos, Obadiah, Jonah, Micah, Nahum, Habakkuk, Zephaniah, Haggai, Zechariah and Malachi.

The Prophet Isaiah

This magnificent poet is the greatest of the prophets and one of the major witnesses of the Messianic hope in Israel. His ministry began in the second half of the 8th century B.C. which saw the collapse of the Northern Kingdom (722) and the constant peril of the Southern Kingdom at the hands of her foes. Isaiah was a man of great vision, ability and political influence whose message is stamped by the majesty, holiness, and glory of the Lord and the pettiness and sinfulness of man. His prophecies concerning Immanuel are most important because of their Messianic character and their influence on Christian revelation.

Isaiah attacked social injustice as that which was most indicative of Judah's tenuous relationship with God. He exhorted his hearers to trust in their omnipotent God and to live accordingly. Thus justice and righteousness, teaching and word, and assurance of divine blessing upon the faithful and

An angel touches Isaiah's lips with an ember.

punishment upon the faithless are recurrent themes of his message from the Holy One of Israel to a proud and stubborn people.

As we have seen, Chapters 40—55 (called Second Isaiah) of his Book are attributed to an anonymous poet who prophesied toward the end of the Babylonian exile. Chapters 56—66 (Third Isaiah) contain oracles from a later period and were composed by disciples who inherited the spirit and continued the work of the great prophet.

The Prophet Jeremiah

Beginning his career reluctantly in 626 B.C., this "prophet of the eleventh hour" had the unpleasant task of predicting the destruction of the Holy City and the Southern Kingdom, and of witnessing these events. He also foretold the return from the Babylonian Exile, and uttered the great oracle of the "New Covenant," sometimes called "the Gospel before the Gospel."

This passage contains his most sublime teaching and is a landmark in Old Testament theology. He continues to urge us today to go beyond a formalistic religion and put in its place

The Lord touches Jeremiah's mouth.

a religion of the heart. Because of his many sufferings for his divine mission, Jeremiah is regarded as a type of Jesus Christ. (For Ezekiel and Daniel, see pp. 58-59.)

THE FOUR EMPIRES

From the time of the reforms effected by Nehemiah and Ezra, the Jewish people came under the rule of four different nations. This lasted until the time of the Maccabees in the second century B.C.

The Persians (538-333 B.C.)

This empire allowed the Jews to live under their own laws. All that was demanded of them was the payment of a small tribute. There was an abundance in town and country, and the people enjoyed peace and tranquility.

The Greeks (333-168 B.C.)

Alexander the Great ended the rule of the Persians. He swept across Asia with his huge army, conquering nations and rulers and bringing them under his dominion. He came to Jerusalem intending to punish the Jews for not submitting to him. However, when he met the High Priest and the citizens of Jerusalem, he changed towards the Jews and permitted them to keep their own laws and customs.

The Egyptians (300-200 B.C.)

After the death of Alexander, the Jews came under the rule of King Ptolemy II of Egypt. Although thousands of Jews were taken captive, they were looked upon favorably. During this king's reign, the Old Testament was translated into Greek. This **Septuagint**, as it is called, was the most important version. It was made necessary because of the dispersion of the Jews and the fact that most of them spoke Greek at that time.

The Jews were under Egyptian rule for over 100 years.

The Syrians (200-135 B.C.)

This empire, under the Seleucid kings, controlled the greater part of Alexander's empire. They soon brought the Jews under subjection and treated them cruelly.

THE MACCABEES (135-36 B.C.)

This name refers to the family of Mattathias, a priest of the house of Aaron and father of five sons: John, Simon, Judas, Eleazar and Jonathan. God raised up these men to fight for the faith of His people during the cruel persecutions under the Seleucid kings.

Mattathias urged the Jews to wage war against the Syrians, who were forcing them to adopt the pagan religion of the Greeks. He exhorted the people to observe all the precepts of the Law and to unite under the guidance of the high priest Simon. Judas Maccabeus was to lead them in battle against their persecutors.

Judas

After his father's death, Judas won several victories. Then he and his brothers proceeded to purify the temple. They tore down the altar, which had been desecrated, and built a new one.

Judas won a complete victory over Nicanor, general of the army of King Demetrius. But he was killed in a later battle and was mourned by all the people. Judas was succeeded by his brothers, Jonathan and Simon the high priest.

The last of the Maccabees to rule was John Hyrcanus, who succeeded Simon as high priest.

Eleazar

Eleazar was a scribe and a staunch defender of the Jewish religion. When he was forced to open his mouth to eat forbidden meat, he spat it out, preferring to go to his death rather than disobey the law of God. Although ninety years old, he went bravely to his martyrdom and was scourged to death.

A mother and her seven sons were put to death in the most brutal manner, the mother encouraging all her sons to remain steadfast.

Doctrinal Notes

In relating the tortures and atrocities committed against those who remained true to their faith, belief in the providence of God is demonstrated. For God often permits great suffering and misfortune, not for our ruin, but as a correction in order to bring us back to Him. God in His own time and manner avenges the wrongs inflicted on the just.

The belief that prayers and sacrifices offered for the dead are beneficial is shown by Judas Maccabeus, when he and his men prayed for those who had been slain and sent an offering to Jerusalem as atonement for the sins of the dead.

JEWISH SECTS AND PARTIES

During these later times, several sects and parties arose and there was much contention among them for political power.

In the meantime, the Romans were steadily advancing in their conquests across Asia Minor. Treaties had been made between the Romans and the Jews during the time of the Maccabees. These alliances were formed to protect those Jews living in the countries outside of their own nation.

In 63 B.C. Jerusalem was captured by Pompey, and Judea came under Roman rule.

The most noted among the Jewish sects were the following:

The **Pharisees**, who thought that the mere knowledge and outward observance of the Law was sufficient to save them from eternal punishment. They believed in the existence of angels, the immortality of the soul and the resurrection of the body. They were proud and sought public attention.

The **Sadducees**, though fewer in number than the Pharisees, were influential because of the wealthy and powerful people belonging to their party. They denied the resurrection of the body and the immortality of the soul.

The **Essenes** were a sort of religious congregation. They were only admitted to the group after a probation and novitiate. They lived a prayerful life and carefully observed the Law. They despised riches, kept silence and showed great reverence to their superiors.

The **Publicans** were tax collectors, often abused their office, and were despised for their injustices.

The **Herodians**, though belonging to the Jewish religion, followed the pagan principles of the Herodian kings.

HEROD (39-4 B.C.)

This king, called "the Great," received his appointment from the Romans. He tried to win the goodwill of the Jews by rebuilding the Temple and erecting public buildings. But he was hated, nevertheless, because of his cruelty and wickedness. He had the last of the Maccabees put to death, and exterminated the Sanhedrin.

FULLNESS OF TIME

And now the fullness of time had come. God would send His Son, born of a woman—the promised and long-awaited Messiah—who would come into the world to redeem men from their sins.

It was about the 34th year of King Herod's reign that Jesus Christ was born, Who came to reign over all the true people of God. He is King and Priest forever, according to the order of Melchizedek, and His kingdom shall have no end.

Our Lord and Savior, Jesus Christ.

I. BIRTH AND EARLY LIFE (7-6 B.C. to 27 A.D.)

ST. JOHN THE BAPTIST

During the reign of King Herod, there was a priest by the name of Zechariah, belonging to the priestly class of Abijah. His wife, Elizabeth, was a descendant of Aaron. They were just in the eyes of God and faithfully followed His Commandments. They had no children, for Elizabeth was unable to bear a child, and both were advanced in age.

One day, when it was Zechariah's turn to carry out his priestly functions, according to custom, he entered the sanctuary of the Lord to offer incense. A great number of people were praying outside during that hour. An angel of the Lord appeared to Zechariah, standing at the right side of the altar of incense. Zechariah was frightened, but the angel reassured him and informed Zechariah that Elizabeth would have a son whom they were to name John. This child would bring them great joy and many would rejoice at his birth.

The angel then told Zechariah that his son was to be the forerunner of the Lord, and that he would be filled with the Holy Spirit from his mother's womb. He would drink no wine or strong drink, and God Himself would go before him in the spirit and power of Elijah to convert the hearts of many and to prepare a people favorable to the Lord.

Zechariah asked how he was to know this since both he and his wife were elderly. The angel announced that his name was Gabriel, one who stood before the throne of God. He also told Zechariah that he would be mute until the child's birth because he had doubted.

Meantime, the people waiting outside wondered why Zechariah was so long in the Temple. When he came out he was unable to speak and they understood that he had seen a vision. The son born to Zechariah and Elizabeth was St. John the Baptist.

THE ANNUNCIATION

After six months, the Angel Gabriel was again sent by God to a humble virgin at Nazareth, in the province of Galilee. The virgin's name was Mary and she was betrothed to a man named Joseph of the house of David. The angel greeted her in the words of the "Hail Mary." He announced to the holy virgin that she was chosen to be the mother of God and that she would have this Child by the power of the Holy Spirit. He also told her of the son soon to be born to her cousin Elizabeth.

The Angel Gabriel greets the Virgin Mary.

Mary replied to the angel in words that are recalled by the prayer called the "Angelus": "I am the servant of the Lord. Let it be done to me according to your word."

Mary visits Elizabeth and Zechariah.

THE VISITATION

Then Mary set out at once to visit her cousin in the hill country of Judah. When she entered Zechariah's house she greeted Elizabeth. As soon as Elizabeth heard Mary's greeting, the baby leaped in her womb and Elizabeth was filled with the Holy Spirit. Crying out with a loud voice, she said to Mary: "Blessed are you among women and blessed is the fruit of your womb. But who am I that the mother of my Lord should come to me?"

Then the Blessed Virgin Mary replied to her in a beautiful canticle, praising God and proclaiming His greatness. This canticle is known as the **Magnificat**. Mary stayed with Elizabeth about three months and returned to her home.

DREAM OF ST. JOSEPH

Meanwhile, St. Joseph did not know the mystery surrounding the Child that our Blessed Lady was bearing. He did not want to expose her publicly to the Law and thought of divorcing her quietly. But an angel appeared to him in sleep

Mary and Joseph with Jesus in the manger.

and told him not to fear, that the Child Mary was carrying in her womb was the Son of God, made flesh through the power of the Holy Spirit. St. Joseph was instructed to call the Child "Jesus," which means "Savior," for He would save His people from their sins.

BIRTH OF OUR LORD

Our Lord Jesus was of the family of David and it was prophesied that He would be born in Bethlehem, the City of David. The providence of God most often uses human instruments to carry out His purposes. In the case of the birth of the Messiah, the instrument was the Roman Emperor, Caesar Augustus. About the time the birth of our Savior was to take place, the Emperor sent out a decree that all the people were to go to the city of their origin to be enrolled. Therefore, Mary and Joseph traveled from Nazareth to Bethlehem to fulfill this order, since both were of the house and family of David.

When they arrived there, weary from their long journey, they found the inns and houses crowded with visitors, and they were turned away from door to door. St. Joseph knew of a cave on the outskirts of the little town and there they went to spend the night and await the birth of the Savior. It was winter. There, in the bare, cold stable, Jesus Christ, second Person of the Most Holy Trinity, was born.

He, Who was God, Creator of heaven and earth, chose to be born as man in the midst of poverty. His cradle was a manger; His warmth only swaddling bands and the breath of the animals who occupied the cave. He could have had a royal palace and all comforts. He deliberately chose poverty and discomfort to show us that things we value so much soon pass away. But what He lacked in material comfort was made up for in the loving adoration of His holy Mother and St. Joseph, who willingly shared His poverty.

ADORATION OF THE SHEPHERDS

In the hills of Bethlehem there were shepherds keeping the night watch over their flocks. An angel of the Lord appeared to them and gave them the message of the birth of Christ, the long-awaited Messiah. Then a whole host of angels were in the heavens, singing the glorious hymn we know so well: "Glory to God in the highest, and peace on earth to those on whom His favor rests." Of course, the shepherds were startled, but the angel calmed their fears and told them where they would find the Infant. Without hesitating, they hurried across the dark fields and found the stable where the Holy Infant lay with Mary His Mother and St. Joseph. They adored their Messiah.

THE CIRCUMCISION

According to the Law of Moses, our Lord was circumcised eight days after His birth. He, Who was sinless, willed to submit to this law for our sakes, for He was to take upon Himself the burden of our sins. As heaven had decreed, the Holy Name of Jesus was given to Him. This Name is above all other names and must be reverenced by all. St. Paul tells us that "at the Name of Jesus every knee should bow, in heaven, on earth, and under the earth."

The newborn babe is circumcised and called Jesus.

Simeon holds Jesus and predicts Mary's sorrow.

THE PRESENTATION

According to the Law of Moses, every firstborn son was to be consecrated to the Lord. Consequently, at the end of the appointed forty days, Mary and Joseph brought the Divine Infant to Jerusalem to present Him in the Temple. They offered two young pigeons in sacrifice, the customary offering of the poor.

There was a holy man named Simeon living in Jerusalem at that time. He longed to see the Lord's Anointed. It was promised to him by the Holy Spirit that he would not die until his desire was fulfilled. Inspired by the Holy Spirit, he came to the Temple when the Child was presented. Taking Him in his arms, he thanked God for this favor. Then Simeon blessed the parents and said to Mary, His Mother: "This Child is destined to be the downfall and the rise of many in Israel, and to be a sign that will be opposed so that the thoughts of many hearts may be revealed. And a sword will pierce your own soul, too."

ADORATION OF THE MAGI

After the birth of Jesus, Wise Men from the East came to Jerusalem to inquire of Herod where the newborn king of the the Jews was to be found. They had followed a new star which appeared in the East and wanted to pay homage to the new king. When Herod was informed by the chief priests and the scribes that the Messiah was to be born in Bethlehem, he told the Wise Men to go there. He asked them to return to him when they had found the Child so that he too might go and offer homage.

The Wise Men worship the Child Jesus and offer Him gifts.

After they left Herod, the star reappeared and led them to where the Child Jesus was. They found Him with Mary, His Mother. Then they offered Him their gifts of gold, frankincense and myrrh. The gift of gold signifies the eternal Kingship of Christ; that of frankincense His Priesthood; the gift of myrrh was symbolic of His Passion and Death on the Cross. The Magi were told in a dream not to return to Herod, so they went back to their own country by a different route.

THE HOLY INNOCENTS

When Herod realized that the Wise Men had not returned, he became very angry. Then he had all the male children under two years of age living in the area of Bethlehem put to death by the sword. This brutal act had been foretold by the prophet Jeremiah.

THE FLIGHT INTO EGYPT

During the night, the angel of the Lord appeared to St. Joseph and told him of Herod's wicked plan to take the life of Jesus. "Get up, take the Child and His Mother, and escape to Egypt," the angel said. St. Joseph obeyed at once.

An angel warns Joseph in a dream to flee to Egypt.

Furthermore, St. Joseph had to find work when they arrived in that strange country. This shows us that God often tries those He loves and who love Him in order to bring them closer to Him. The Holy Family stayed in Egypt until the death of Herod. When they returned, they settled in Nazareth of Galilee. This fulfilled the prophecy that our Lord would be called a Nazorean.

LOSS OF JESUS

Every year the Blessed Virgin and St. Joseph went to Jerusalem to celebrate the Passover feast. When our Lord was twelve years old He went with them. After the feast, Jesus remained in Jerusalem, unknown to His parents. Mary and Joseph looked for Him among their relatives and friends, and not finding Him, returned to Jerusalem. On the third day they found Him in the Temple, listening to the doctors of the law and asking them questions.

The Boy Jesus amazes the teachers in the Temple.

He then returned to Nazareth with His parents and was obedient to them. His Mother kept all these things in her heart. Jesus, for His part, progressed steadily in wisdom and age and grace before God and men.

THE HIDDEN LIFE

Our Lord remained at Nazareth until His thirtieth year. During this time He prepared for His public life by prayer and work. He learned the carpentry trade from His foster-father, St. Joseph. It is generally believed that St. Joseph died while

Jesus was living at home. Joseph's work was finished. He had been honored by being chosen to be the father to God's Son in the eyes of the people. He had protected and loved Him through His childhood. This holy patriarch died a saintly death in the presence of Jesus and Mary. The Church has designated him patron of a happy death.

II. PUBLIC MINISTRY (27 to 30 A.D.)

BAPTISM OF JESUS

Meanwhile, St. John the Baptist was living a life of prayer and penance in the desert. He was dressed in camel's hair and wore a leather belt around his waist. His food consisted of locusts and wild honey.

The word of God was spoken to him, and he preached a baptism of repentance throughout the entire area of the Jordan. Many people came to him asking to be baptized. He was truly the forerunner of the Messiah, fulfilling the prophecy of Isaiah to make straight the way of the Lord, and that all mankind would see the salvation of God.

John preaches a baptism of repentance at the Jordan.

When John was questioned by the Pharisees, he told them that he was not the Messiah and that One more powerful than he was to come after him, whose sandal strap he was not worthy to untie. St. John the Baptist gave witness that Jesus was "the Lamb of God Who takes away the sin of the world."

One day, our Lord Jesus came to him and asked to be baptized. While John was performing this rite, the Holy Spirit descended upon our Lord in the form of a dove. Then a voice from heaven was heard to say: "This is My beloved Son with Whom I am well pleased."

When St. John saw the Holy Spirit descend upon Jesus, he said: "Now I have seen for myself and have testified, 'This is God's chosen One.'"

Jesus is baptized by John.

IN THE DESERT

After His baptism, our Lord went into the desert, where He fasted for forty days. We commemorate this fast of Christ in our observance of the forty days of Lent. At the end of this period, Satan came to tempt Him. Knowing He was hungry, the devil first suggested that our Lord change the stones into bread, if He were the Son of God. Jesus said to him: "It is written, 'Not on bread alone shall man live, but on every word that comes from the mouth of God.' "

Satan next set Him on the pinnacle of the Temple and told Him, if He were the Son of God, to throw Himself down, because it is written that God will send His angels to support Him. But Jesus answered him: "It is also written, 'You shall not put the Lord your God to the test.' "

Finally, the devil took Him to a very high mountain and showed Him all the kingdoms of the world. Satan offered to give Jesus all of these if He would fall down and adore him. Then Jesus said to him: "Away with you, Satan! For it is written: 'You shall do homage to the Lord your God, and Him alone shall you serve.' " Then the devil left Him and angels came and waited on Him.

THE FIRST DISCIPLES

When St. John the Baptist told some of his followers that Jesus was the Messiah, two of his disciples left him to follow our Lord. One of these was Andrew, who immediately sought out his brother Simon and told him they had found the Messiah. When Simon came to Jesus, He said to him: "You are Simon, son of John; your name shall be Cephas" (which means Peter—or rock).

Later, as He walked by the Sea of Galilee, He saw Peter and Andrew fishing. He simply said to them: "Come after Me and I will make you fishers of men." They left their nets and became His followers. Then He came upon the two sons of Zebedee, James and John. They, too, were fishermen, and He called them also to follow Him. They left their father and their boat and went with Him.

The next day, Jesus continued on His way with His little band of followers. He first met Philip and said to him: "Follow Me." Philip found his friend, Nathanael or Bartholomew

Jesus calls Andrew and John to follow Him.

(son of Tholmai), and told him the good news that they had found the Messiah. When Nathanael was persuaded to come, Jesus showed that He knew him. Nathanael's immediate response was: "Rabbi, You are the Son of God; You are the King of Israel."

As He continued through Galilee, He saw a tax collector named Matthew, or Levi, sitting at his customs post. He told him also to follow Him. Levi left his post at once and went with Him. In the call of the various disciples we see how necessary it is for those who are chosen to be fishers of men to follow God's call promptly, without considering what they must give up.

MARRIAGE AT CANA

Jesus and His disciples were invited to a wedding at Cana in Galilee, and the Mother of Jesus was there. She observed that the supply of wine was low and she told Jesus about it. Although our Lord replied that His hour had not yet come, Mary instructed the waiters to do whatever He told them to do. At this request of His Mother, Jesus changed water into wine. This was His first public miracle. So did He reveal His power and His disciples believed in Him. And

Jesus tells the attendants to fill the jars with water.

so do we understand the power of our Blessed Mother's intercession.

THE CLEANSING OF THE TEMPLE

The Jewish feast of the Passover was drawing near, and Jesus went up to Jerusalem. When He entered the Temple, He saw some of the people engaged in buying and selling animals and others at tables exchanging coins. Making a whip of cords tied together, He drove the people and the animals from the Temple area. He turned over the tables of the money-changers, spilling their coins. He told those who sold the doves and pigeons to take them away, saying: "Stop turning My Father's house into a marketplace!" The words of the psalmist were fulfilled: "Zeal for Your house will consume Me."

The Jews asked Him what sign He could show them of His authority to do these things. Jesus replied: "Destroy this Temple, and in three days I will raise it up." He was prophesying the resurrection of His Body.

Jesus drives the buyers and sellers from the Temple.

NICODEMUS

While Jesus was in Jerusalem, a Pharisee named Nicodemus came at night to talk to Him. Our Lord told him of the necessity of baptism in order to gain heaven, saying: "Amen, amen, I say to you, no one can enter God's kingdom unless he is born of water and Spirit." Our Lord also told Nicodemus that it was necessary to believe that God sent His only Son to save the world; that whoever believes in the Son will be saved, but that whoever does not believe in Him is already condemned.

SAMARIA

Our Lord now left Judea to return to Galilee. It was necessary to pass through Samaria on His journey. Since its captivity by the Assyrians this province had been inhabited by the pagan Babylonians. These intermingled with the old inhabitants, some of whom had returned after the captivity. Together they formed one people, called Samaritans. Although they strictly observed the Mosaic Law and looked for the Messiah Who would teach all truth, they did not acknowledge much of the traditional doctrine held by the Jews. They disowned the Temple at Jerusalem and the priesthood, setting up their own rival place of worship on Mount Gerizim. For these reasons they were looked down upon and hated by the Jews.

Jesus paused in His journey to rest at Jacob's well in Shechem and sent His disciples to a neighboring town to buy provisions. At that hour a woman came to the well to draw water. Our Lord asked her for a drink and engaged her in conversation. He revealed to her His knowledge of her life and the woman acknowledged Him as a prophet. Jesus informed her that her people worshiped what they did not understand, while the Jews understood what they worshiped, for salvation was to come through the Jews.

He then told her that the time was at hand when the real worshipers would adore the Father in Spirit and in truth. The woman told Him of her belief in the Messiah Who was to come. Our Lord answered her: "I Who speak to you am He." This first revelation of His divinity Jesus made to this stranger of Samaria. In this we see that though He was born of the Jewish race, our Lord was sent to save all those who would believe in Him and accept His teaching.

When the disciples returned, they were surprised to find Jesus speaking with the Samaritan woman. When they urged Him to eat something, He explained that His food was to do the will of His Father. Many of the Samaritans believed in Him because of the woman's word. These people urged Jesus to stay with them. So He remained two days and many more came to believe in Him through His teaching. They told the woman: "No longer does our faith depend on what you told us. We have heard for ourselves, and we know that this Man really is the Savior of the world."

This woman was a real missionary to her own people. She herself believed and spoke of the Messiah to the others, bringing them to Him.

THE RULER'S SON

After His stay in Samaria, Jesus journeyed to Galilee, and came again to Cana, where He had changed the water into wine. There was a certain royal official at Capernaum who came to Him, asking that He cure his son who was dying. This man recognized the authority of our Lord, for he told Him that it was not necessary to come down to his house to cure his son. He needed only to say the word and the boy would be cured.

Jesus told the ruler to go on his way, that his son would live. The man believed the word of Jesus and his whole household believed also. Then Jesus spoke to the crowd following Him and praised the faith of the official which was far greater than that of many of the Jews. The words of this official's act of faith are those which we say before receiving Communion.

Jesus tells the royal official that his son will live.

PREACHING AT NAZARETH

The reputation of Jesus spread throughout Galilee, not only on account of the miraculous cures He performed, but because He taught with authority. When He came to His own town of Nazareth, He entered the synagogue on the sabbath day and began to read from the Prophet Isaiah, written in the scroll handed to Him. He told those present that the text referred to Himself; that He was the Messiah in Whom those words were fulfilled.

Our Lord reminded the people that a prophet is not accepted in his own town. He could not perform the miracles there that He did in Capernaum because of their lack of faith. Then the people became very angry and would have thrown Him over the edge of the hill on which the town was built. But He passed through the midst of them and went away.

MIRACULOUS DRAUGHT OF FISH

One day, by the Lake of Gennesaret, when the crowd pressed in on Jesus, He got into Simon Peter's boat to preach to them. After He had finished, He asked Simon to pull out into the deep water and to cast his net for a catch of fish. Simon told Jesus that he and his men had been fishing all night but had caught nothing. However, at our Lord's request they lowered the net and caught so many fish that they had to call on their partners in another boat to come to help them.

When Simon Peter saw this, he fell at the feet of Jesus, saying: "Depart from me, Lord. I am a sinful man." All the disciples were amazed at the catch. Jesus reassured Simon that from then on he would catch men.

SABBATH AT CAPERNAUM

When our Lord was in the synagogue at Capernaum with His disciples, a man appeared there who had an unclean

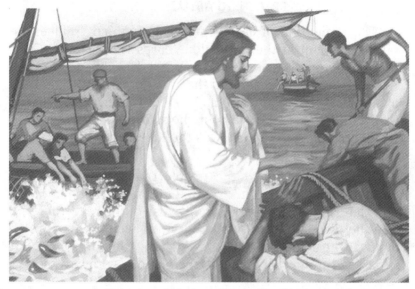

Peter kneels in humility before Jesus.

spirit. The demon shrieked, and Jesus commanded him to be silent and to come out of the man. Throwing the man into a convulsion and shrieking loudly, the spirit came out of him. After this, our Lord's fame spread throughout Galilee.

When He left the synagogue, Jesus came to the house of Simon and Andrew. Simon's mother-in-law was ill with a fever. Jesus simply took her by the hand and the fever left her. Then she got up and waited on them.

Before long, many brought their sick to be healed by Him. He cured them of their various diseases and cast out demons from those who were possessed.

THE PARALYTIC

On one of the days when Jesus was teaching, He also healed many sick who were brought to Him, for the power of God was with Him. Pharisees and teachers of the law had gathered from the villages of Galilee and Judea and even from Jerusalem.

Then came some men carrying a paralytic on a mat. When they saw the crowd around our Lord, they removed some of the tiles from the roof and lowered the sick man down, laying him in front of Jesus. When He saw their faith, He said to the sick man: "Your sins are forgiven you."

Immediately the scribes and Pharisees raised a question and accused Him of blasphemy. For they said to themselves:

Jesus tells the paralytic to rise and return home.

"Who can forgive sins but God alone?" Jesus knew their reasoning. In order that they and all present would know that the Son of Man had power to forgive sins, He told the sick man to get up, take up his mat and return home. All were astonished at what they had seen and, filled with awe, they gave praise to God.

CURE ON A SABBATH FEAST

The time of a Jewish feast was coming around, and Jesus again went up to Jerusalem. There was a Sheep Pool that in

Hebrew was called Bethesda. Many sick people were lying there waiting to be put into the pool when the water was stirred up. One man had waited 38 years, afflicted with his infirmity. When our Lord saw him, He had compassion on him and cured him. It was a sabbath.

When certain Jewish officials saw the man carrying his mat and knew that he had been ill a long time, they questioned him. The man did not know that it was Jesus Who had cured him. Later, Jesus met him near the Temple and told him that he must give up his sins or some worse fate would befall him. The man then informed the officials that Jesus was the One Who had cured him.

These people then began to persecute our Lord because He healed on the sabbath. But Jesus told them that He did the same work as His Father. God has power over life and death, and is Lord of the sabbath. The Son has the same power as the Father. His opponents then were determined to kill Him, not only because in their eyes He broke the sabbath, but because He spoke of God as His Father.

There was another sabbath when Jesus healed a man who had a withered hand. He was in the synagogue and told the man to stand up and stretch out his hand. Jesus healed him, and the Pharisees were furious and began to plot how they could destroy Him.

CHOOSING THE APOSTLES

One day, our Lord went up into a mountain and spent the night in prayer. This He often did. When daybreak came, He called His disciples together and selected twelve of them to be His apostles. These were: Simon, whom He named Peter, Andrew, his brother, James and John, Philip and Bartholomew, Matthew and Thomas, James son of Alphaeus, Simon of the Zealot party, Thaddeus, and Judas Iscariot, who betrayed Him.

SERMON ON THE MOUNT

As His fame spread, many came to Him from all over Galilee and Judea, and even from beyond the Jordan. They brought their sick to be healed and He expelled the demons from those who were possessed. When Jesus saw the crowds, He went up on a mountainside. His disciples gathered around Him and He began to teach them. It is in this well-known Sermon on the Mount that our Divine Lord gave His hearers and us the Eight Beatitudes. In these are contained the whole morality of the Gospel.

To follow the teaching of Christ is not easy, but in this beautiful discourse our Lord shows us how blest are they who do. Furthermore, He holds out to those who love Him the reward for doing so—and that reward is not something temporary. It will last forever.

Jesus teaches the New Law to the people.

Jesus tells His followers that they are the salt of the earth and the light of the world. They are to act in such a way that they set a good example to others and so give glory to God. Our Lord further tells us how we are to pray in private, and He gives us the most perfect prayer, the "Our Father." We must persevere in our prayers and not grow discouraged if they are not answered immediately.

He warns us about placing too great value on earthly possessions. It is better to lay up treasure in heaven. We should not be anxious about tomorrow. Do God's will each day and He will take care of us always.

Lastly, we must never judge others. No matter how their actions seem to us, we cannot know the hearts of others and their intentions. This is known only to God.

After this discourse, all the crowd were in admiration at His teaching. He taught with authority and not like their scribes.

THE STORM ON THE LAKE

After the Sermon on the Mount, great crowds followed our Lord when He came down from the mountain. A leper appeared before Him and, after offering Him homage, said to Him: "If you are willing, Lord, you can cure me." "I am willing," answered Jesus. He touched the man and immediately the leprosy left him.

Jesus performed many other miracles. Then He got into the boat with His disciples to cross to the other side of the lake. Suddenly a violent storm arose and the boat was being swamped by the waves. But Jesus was sleeping soundly. The disciples awakened Him, crying out: "Lord, save us! We are going to drown." Jesus stood up and commanded the waves to cease, and the sea became calm. He took the disciples to task for their lack of courage. "How little faith you have," He said. The men were overcome with awe and said: "What

Jesus calms the wind and the waves.

kind of Man is this? Even the winds and the waves obey
Him!"

LEGION OF DEVILS

On reaching the other side of the lake, they came to the
territory of the Gerasenes. When they landed, a man met them
who was possessed by demons. He lived among the tombs
and not even chains were able to restrain him. When he saw
Jesus, he fell at His feet, shrieking: "What do You want with
me, Jesus, Son of God Most High? Do not torment me, I beg
You!"

Jesus commanded the demons to be silent and to come
out of the man. "What is your name?" He asked them. "Legion,"
he answered, for the demons who had entered him were
many. When ordering them to leave the man, He gave them
permission to enter a herd of swine. When they did, the whole
herd rushed into the sea and were drowned.

When the townspeople arrived, they found the possessed man fully clothed and sitting calmly at the feet of Jesus. They were seized with fear at this sight and asked Jesus to leave their land. The man who was cured begged our Lord to be allowed to return with Him. But Jesus refused his request and instructed him to return to his people and tell them all that God had done for him. This the man did and all were amazed at his account.

THE DAUGHTER OF JAIRUS

Jesus and His disciples returned in the boat to the opposite shore. One of the rulers of the synagogue, named Jairus, came to Him, begging Him to come to heal his little daughter who was critically ill.

A great crowd followed and among them was a woman who had been afflicted with an incurable hemorrhage for twelve years. She touched His cloak, firmly believing that this was sufficient to heal her. Immediately the bleeding stopped. Our Lord was aware that power had gone out from Him. He looked around to see who had touched Him. The woman

Jesus raises the daughter of Jairus.

came forward and fell at His feet, telling Him her whole story. He assured her that it was her faith that had cured her and to go in peace.

As they reached the ruler's house, word came to them that the little girl was dead. When Jesus went into the house all the people were wailing. He told them that the girl was not dead, but they laughed at Him. Then entering the child's room with her parents and the three disciples, Peter, James and John, He took the girl by the hand and said to her: "Little girl, get up." Immediately she stood up and He told her parents to give her some food.

MISSION OF THE SEVENTY-TWO

Soon Jesus appointed seventy-two disciples and called them to Him. He sent them out in pairs to announce the reign of God. He gave them power to cast out devils and to cure diseases. He also told them: "He who hears you, hears Me. He who rejects you, rejects Me. And he who rejects Me, rejects Him Who sent Me."

Jesus sends the seventy-two disciples to preach the reign of God.

THE WIDOW'S SON

During His journeys through Galilee, Jesus came to the town of Nain. There He met the funeral procession of a young man, the only son of a widowed mother. Noticing the poor woman's grief, His heart was moved with pity. So He ordered the stretcher bearers to stop. Then He said to the dead man: "Young man, I say to you, get up." Immediately the dead man sat up and began to speak, and Jesus gave him back

Jesus raises the widow's son.

to his mother. Needless to say, the people were filled with awe, and the report of it spread throughout the countryside.

THE PENITENT WOMAN

One day, a Pharisee by the name of Simon invited Jesus to dine with him. While they were at dinner, a woman who had a bad reputation in the town entered the house and stood behind Jesus. She began to weep, and her tears fell on His feet and she wiped them with her hair. Then she anointed them with perfumed oil. Our Divine Lord knew her sorrow and repentance, and said to her: "Your sins are forgiven. Your faith has been your salvation. Go in peace."

Turning to His host, Jesus reminded the Pharisee that he had not performed the customary courtesies due to a guest and that this woman had supplied them by her tears and her anointing of His feet. Jesus knew that Simon had wondered within himself if Jesus knew the kind of woman He permitted to touch Him. Much is forgiven those whose love is great.

THE WOMEN WHO SERVED

As our Lord journeyed from village to village preaching the Gospel of the kingdom, some of the women who had been cured of maladies and evil spirits followed Him and His disciples. Mary called the Magdalene, from whom seven devils had gone out, was one of them, as well as Joanna, the wife of Chuza, who was Herod's steward, Susanna, and many others. These women were devoted to looking after the needs of Jesus and His disciples, and in helping them with the means at their disposal.

CHRIST'S TESTIMONY TO ST. JOHN THE BAPTIST

While Jesus was preaching throughout the towns, John the Baptist had been imprisoned by Herod. St. John had told Herod that it was sinful for him to take his brother's wife.

When John heard all the works that our Lord was performing, he sent some of his disciples to find out whether He was truly the Christ, or whether they were to wait for another. When Jesus had reassured them and sent them back to John, He spoke to the assembled people about St. John. He said that he was a prophet—even more than a prophet; for John had fulfilled the Scripture, which says: "I will send My messenger ahead of You to prepare Your way before You."

THE BEHEADING OF ST. JOHN

Twice during his ministry as forerunner of the Messiah, John the Baptist had borne testimony to Him. Now he was to give his final witness by surrendering his life for the principles pronounced by Christ.

Because of a rash promise made to a dancing girl, who pleased Herod by her performance at his birthday celebration, Herod sent his men to behead St. John in prison.

FIVE THOUSAND FED MIRACULOUSLY

The disciples returned from the mission on which Jesus had sent them full of enthusiasm. They reported to Him all they had accomplished. He decided to retire with them to a quiet place across the lake where they could rest a little. The people soon learned where they were going and when they reached their destination they found a huge crowd waiting for them.

Our Lord had compassion on these people, for they were like sheep without a shepherd. So He taught them and healed their sick. As evening approached, the disciples suggested that He dismiss the crowd so that they could find food in the villages. Jesus said to them: "Give them something to eat yourselves." They informed Him that there was nothing available but five barley loaves and a couple of dried fish, and asked where would they get money to buy food for so many.

Jesus then told them to have the people sit down in groups. There were about five thousand men, not counting the women and children. Then He took the loaves and the fish and, raising His eyes to heaven, He blessed them and gave them to the disciples to distribute among the people. When they had eaten all they desired, He told the disciples to gather up what was left over so that nothing would be wasted. They filled twelve baskets with the remaining fragments.

Jesus gives thanks over five loaves and two fish.

The crowd was in great admiration of this miracle. Our Lord realized that they would try to make Him king, so He went to the mountain alone to pray.

JESUS WALKS ON THE WATER

In the meantime, the disciples got into the boat to cross the lake and return to Capernaum. When they were a long distance from shore, Jesus saw that the wind was against them and that they were having a hard time rowing. So He came walking on the water toward them. At first they thought He was a ghost, and they cried out in fear. "It is I; do not be afraid," He said.

Then Peter spoke up and said to Him: "Lord, if it is you, tell me to come to You across the water." "Come!" Jesus said. Peter got out of the boat and began to walk on the water toward Jesus. But when he looked at the waves, he lost confidence and immediately began to sink. "Lord, save me!" he cried out. Jesus held out His hand and caught him, saying: "How little faith you have! Why did you doubt?"

THE BREAD OF LIFE

After the multiplication of the loaves, the next day the crowd realized that our Lord and His disciples were on the other side of the lake. Therefore they too crossed over and went to Capernaum in search of Jesus. They asked Him when He had come there. Jesus answered them that He knew they were looking for Him not because of the signs they had seen but because they had eaten of the loaves. He told them that He would give them food for eternal life and that they must have faith in the One Whom God had sent. Before they would put their faith in Him, they asked Him for a sign of the work He was to perform for them. They recalled that Moses had given their ancestors bread from the heavens.

Jesus promises the Holy Eucharist.

Jesus explained to them that it was God Who gave the real heavenly bread. God's bread comes down from heaven and gives life to the world. "I am the Bread of Life," He told them. "No one who comes to Me shall ever be hungry, and no one who believes in Me shall ever thirst."

The people knew our Lord only as the carpenter's son, and questioned how He could claim to have come down from heaven. Jesus told them again: "I am the Living Bread come down from heaven. The bread I will give is My Flesh for the life of the world." They argued among themselves as to how He could give them His Flesh to eat. Then Jesus explained to them that His Flesh was real food and His Blood real drink. "He who eats My Flesh and drinks My Blood has life eternal, and I will raise him up on the last day," He said.

Many of His disciples would not accept these words, and Jesus knew that they were protesting against what He said. After that, many of them no longer followed Him. But our Lord did not take back what He had said, for it was the truth. He only turned to the Twelve and asked them if they too wanted to leave Him. Simon Peter answered Him: "Lord, to whom shall we go? You have the words of eternal life. We have come to believe; we are convinced that You are God's Holy One."

THE CANAANITE WOMAN

When Jesus was journeying through Tyre and Sidon, a Gentile woman—a Syro-Phoenician—came to Him, imploring Him to rid her daughter of a demon. Although He told her that His mission was only to the lost sheep of Israel, she persisted in her plea. She paid Him homage and said: "Help me, Lord!"

Jesus appeared to be harsh with her, even telling her that it was not good to take food from the children and give it to the dogs. But the woman replied: "Please, Lord, even the dogs eat the crumbs that fall from their masters' tables." Jesus, seeing her great faith even in the face of apparent refusal, replied: "Woman, you have great faith! The demon has already left your daughter." When she arrived home, she found the girl lying in bed and the demon was gone.

THE DEAF AND DUMB MAN

Jesus then returned to the Sea of Galilee and was preaching in the district of the Ten Cities. Some people brought Him a deaf-mute and begged Him to heal him. Our Lord had pity on the poor man and took him aside from the crowd. Putting His fingers into the man's ears and spitting, He touched his tongue. He looked up to heaven and groaned. Then He said to him: "Ephphatha!" (which means, "Be opened!"). Immediately the man heard and could speak plainly.

Jesus cures the deaf-mute.

FOUR THOUSAND FED MIRACULOUSLY

Large crowds of people kept coming to Jesus, bringing with them their blind, crippled, deaf, and those with various kinds of ailments. They stayed with Him even in the desert to listen to His words. Our Lord had great compassion for this crowd, who had remained with Him for three days and now had nothing to eat. So He called His disciples to Him and asked them what provisions they had with them. He did not wish to send the people away for fear they would collapse on the way.

The disciples told Him that they had seven loaves and a few small fish. Jesus ordered the crowd to be seated, blessed the loaves and the fish and gave them to His disciples to distribute to the people. After they had eaten their fill, seven baskets of leftovers were left, and the crowd numbered about four thousand, apart from women and children.

On each of the occasions when Jesus fed the multitudes, He first prayed and then blessed the food. Then He told His disciples to feed the people. This is a type of the Holy Eucharist, with which our Lord feeds His people even today.

PETER'S CONFESSION OF FAITH

When our Lord came to the neighborhood of Caesarea Philippi, He asked His disciples: "Who do people say that the Son of Man is?" They replied that some said He was John the Baptist, others Elijah, still others Jeremiah or one of the prophets. Then He asked them: "Who do you say that I am?" And Simon Peter answered: "You are the Messiah, the Son of the living God." Jesus said to him: "Blessed are you, Simon son of Jonah! No mere man has revealed this to you, but My heavenly Father! I for My part declare to you: you are 'Peter,' and on this rock I will build My Church, and the gates of the netherworld shall not prevail against it. I will entrust to you the keys of the kingdom of heaven. Whatever you declare bound on earth shall be bound in heaven; whatever you declare loosed on earth shall be loosed in heaven." Here, Christ, the Founder of His Church, is building His house (His Church) upon a rock, like the wise builder, so that when the rains fall and the winds blow, the house will stand firm against the

Peter declares that Jesus is the Messiah.

storms. The Pope is the successor of St. Peter and the Vicar of Christ on earth.

THE TRANSFIGURATION

After Peter's declaration of faith, our Lord began to instruct them that He, the Messiah, must go up to Jerusalem and suffer many things. He would be rejected by the chief priests and the scribes and be put to death; but He would rise on the third day.

Then Jesus took Peter, James and John up to a high mountain. There He was transfigured before them. His face shone like the sun and His clothing became dazzling white. Then Moses and Elijah appeared and talked with Him. Peter spoke up, saying: "Lord, how good that we are here! With Your permission I will erect three booths here, one for You, one for Moses, and one for Elijah." Scarcely had he said this, when a bright cloud overshadowed them, and a voice was heard

Jesus is transfigured before Peter, James and John.

from the cloud, saying: "This is My beloved Son, with Whom I am well pleased. Listen to Him."

Overcome with fear, the disciples fell with their faces to the ground. Then Jesus came over to them, telling them not to be afraid. Looking up, they saw no one, but only Jesus. Coming down from the mountain, He strictly ordered them not to tell the vision to anyone until the Son of Man had risen from the dead.

A POSSESSED BOY

At the foot of the mountain, they saw a crowd gathered, and a man came up and knelt before Jesus. He implored Him to take pity on his demented son, who was in a serious condition. The boy was possessed by a demon which sometimes threw him into a fire and sometimes into water. The man further stated that he had brought the boy to the disciples but they were unable to do anything for him. Jesus rebuked the crowd for their lack of faith.

Then He ordered the boy to be brought before Him. As soon as the demon caught sight of Jesus, he threw the poor boy into convulsions. The father told Jesus that if He could do anything to help the boy, he would be grateful. Jesus answered him: " 'If you can'? Everything is possible to a man who believes." Humbled, the poor father answered: "I do believe! Help my unbelief!" Then Jesus commanded the evil spirit to leave the boy and not to enter him again. The demon obeyed, throwing the boy into another convulsion, so that many thought he was dead. But Jesus took him by the hand and gave him to his father.

Afterward, the disciples asked Him privately why they were unable to cast out the evil spirit. Jesus explained: "This kind you can drive out only by prayer."

Journeying through Galilee, Jesus again instructed His disciples that the Son of Man would be delivered into the hands of sinful men, who would put Him to death. On the third day He would rise from the dead. But they failed to understand Him.

PAYING THE TEMPLE TAX

When they entered Capernaum, those charged with collecting the temple tax came to Peter to ask if his master paid the tax for the service of the Temple. Peter said that of course his master did. Our Lord then asked Peter a question: "Do the kings of the world take duty and taxes from their sons, or from foreigners?" When Peter answered, "From foreigners," Jesus replied: "Then their sons are exempt." However, in order not to disedify the tax collectors, He told Peter to go to the lake and fish. In the mouth of the first fish he caught he would find a coin which would pay the tax for both of them. And so Peter did.

FEAST OF BOOTHS

Although Jesus had remained mostly in Galilee, because the leaders of the people sought to kill Him, when the Feast of

Booths came He went up to Jerusalem alone. There was much controversy among the crowd, some saying that He was a good man, and others saying that He was misleading the people.

On the last day of the festival, Jesus cried out: "If anyone thirsts, let him come to Me and drink. Whoever believes in Me, as Scripture has it: 'From within him rivers of living waters shall flow.' " Many in the crowd believed in Him. The Pharisees wanted to take Him prisoner, but no one dared to lay hands on Him.

Some of the guards remarked: "No one ever spoke the way this Man does." Even Nicodemus, a member of the Pharisees (the one who came to Jesus at night), said to them: "Since when does our law condemn any man without first hearing him to find out what He is doing?" But the Pharisees were so blinded by their jealousy and hatred that they dismissed him with sarcastic remarks.

THE ADULTERESS

After these events, Jesus went to the Mount of Olives to pray. The next morning He returned to the Temple and was teaching the people. The scribes and Pharisees appeared on the scene, bringing with them a woman who had been caught in adultery, and they stood her before Jesus. They wanted to trap Him in His speech. So they reminded Him that the law of Moses commanded that such a woman should be stoned.

Our Lord did not answer them. Instead, He bent down and started writing on the ground with His finger. Then He told them: "Let the man among you who has no sin be the first to cast a stone at her." Again He bent down and wrote on the ground. One by one the Pharisees drifted away, leaving the woman standing alone before our Lord. Jesus asked her: "Has no one condemned you?" When she answered Him: "No one,

Sir," He told her that neither did He condemn her. He told her to go and avoid that sin in the future.

THE TEN LEPERS

On one of His journeys through Samaria and Galilee, ten lepers came out to meet Jesus. They called out to Him: "Jesus, Master, have pity on us!" He simply told them to show themselves to the priests. On their way, they were cleansed of their disease. One of them realized that he had been cured and returned to thank Jesus and give praise to God. This man was a Samaritan. Jesus remarked that only this foreigner came back to thank God, although all ten were cleansed.

How often we ask favors of God, but give little thought to thanking Him after all He does for us. Gratitude is a virtue pleasing to God.

JESUS BLESSES THE LITTLE CHILDREN

The people were bringing their young children to Jesus that He might place His hands on them. The disciples object-

The Samaritan thanks Jesus for curing his leprosy.

ed to this and wanted to send them away. But our Lord severely scolded them and told them that they must not prevent them from coming. "The Kingdom of God belongs to such as these," He said. Then He embraced them and blessed the little ones, placing His hands on their heads.

ZACCHAEUS

In the city of Jericho lived a rich man by the name of Zacchaeus. He was the chief tax collector of that place. When he heard that Jesus was to pass through the town, he was curious to see Him. Since Zacchaeus was a very short man, he ran on ahead and climbed a sycamore tree so that he could observe Jesus as He came along.

When Jesus came to where this man was perched, He looked up and bid him come down at once, for He wanted to dine at his house. Zacchaeus was beside himself with joy and hurried to carry out his duties as host. Some in the crowd complained that our Lord was going to a sinner's house. But Zacchaeus, touched by divine grace, said to our Lord: "I give half my belongings, Lord, to the poor. If I have defrauded anyone in the least, I pay him back fourfold." Jesus replied: "Today salvation has come to this house, because this man too is a son of Abraham. For the Son of Man has come to seek and to save what was lost." This is what true repentance for sins means.

THE MAN BORN BLIND

One day, our Lord came upon a man who had been blind from birth. His disciples asked Him whether it was his parents' sin or his own that had caused his blindness. Jesus replied that it was no sin at all. It was to let God's works show forth in him. Then He spat on the ground and making a paste of the mud and saliva, He spread it on the man's eyes. He told him to wash in the pool of Siloam. The man did so and returned able to see.

It was on a sabbath that Jesus performed this miracle. When the Pharisees heard of it, they began to question the man, telling him that the One Who cured him was a sinner because He broke the sabbath rule. The man replied: "He is a prophet." He further told the Pharisees that never was it known that a man born blind had been cured. The Pharisees accused Jesus of being a sinner. But the cured man stood his ground firmly. "If this Man were not from God," he told them, "He could never have done such a thing." The Pharisees were furious and threw the man out bodily.

When our Lord heard of this expulsion, He sought out the man and asked him: "Do you believe in the Son of Man?" The man answered Him: "Who is He, Sir? Tell me that I may believe in Him." "You have now seen Him," Jesus replied. "In fact, it is He Who is speaking to you." The man said: "I do believe, Lord," and bowed down to worship Him.

This man who was born blind shows us the courage we must have to stand up for our faith, even at great inconvenience.

THE QUESTION OF DIVORCE

While He was in the Jordan area, Jesus taught the people who gathered around Him. As usual, there were Pharisees present, whose only purpose was to ensnare Him in His speech. So they asked Him if divorce were permissible. They stated that Moses permitted divorce and the writing of a decree of divorce. Jesus told them that Moses only allowed this because of their stubbornness.

He reminded them that God created male and female, and because of this a man must leave father and mother and cling to his wife. "They are no longer two but one flesh. Therefore, let no man separate what God has joined together." He told His disciples: "Whoever divorces his wife and marries another, commits adultery against her; and if she divorces her husband and marries another, she commits adultery."

LAZARUS RAISED TO LIFE

Lazarus lived in Bethany with his sisters, Mary and Martha. Jesus loved this family and often visited them on His journeys. One day, the sisters sent word to Jesus that Lazarus was very sick. Still Jesus did not go immediately to Bethany, for He said: "This sickness is not to end in death; rather it is for God's glory, that through it the Son of God may be glorified." After two days, Jesus told the disciples that Lazarus was dead and said: "Let us go to him." When they arrived in Bethany, they learned that Lazarus had been in the tomb four days.

Martha said to Jesus: "Lord, if You had been here, my brother would never have died." And Mary, when she fell at the feet of Jesus, said the same. Our Lord told them that He was the resurrection and the life and that whoever believed in Him would never die. Martha replied: "I have come to believe that You are the Messiah, the Son of God."

Then Jesus and His disciples went with Mary and Martha to the tomb of Lazarus. The Jews who were there to console the sisters followed after them. When Jesus came to the tomb, He wept, for He loved Lazarus. Then our Lord directed the stone to be rolled away from the front of the tomb. When this was done, Jesus, lifting up His eyes to heaven, said: "Father, I thank You for having heard Me. I know that You always hear Me, but I have said this for the benefit of the people, that they may believe that You sent Me." Then, crying out with a loud voice, He said: "Lazarus, come out!" The dead man came forth, bound in his burial cloths. Our Lord told them to loose his bands and let him go free.

This manifestation of the power of God caused many of the Jews to believe in Jesus. Others, however, immediately informed the Pharisees of the event. They called a meeting with the Sanhedrin, and it was determined that Jesus must die. This decision of theirs was in fulfillment with God's plan that Jesus would die not only for the Jewish nation, but to gather into one all the dispersed children of God. From that day on they sought an opportunity to kill Him.

JESUS ANOINTED

While Jesus was in Bethany, they gave Him a banquet at which Martha served and Lazarus was at table with Him. Mary brought in a costly perfume and anointed the feet of Jesus and wiped them with her hair. Judas Iscariot, one of the Twelve (who was to betray Him), criticized this act severely. He protested that the ointment should not have been wasted but sold and the money given to the poor. Judas cared nothing for the poor. He was a thief, and because he carried the common purse he wanted the money for himself.

Our Lord announced that the woman had done this as a preparation for His burial. "The poor," He said, "you will always have with you, but Me you will not always have." Furthermore, our Lord said: "Wherever the Gospel is proclaimed throughout the world, what she has done will be told in her memory." This tells us how much our Lord regards even our smallest acts of reverence to His sacred Body, as well as our good works for the poor.

ENTRY INTO JERUSALEM

Jesus continued on His journey toward Jerusalem, entering Bethpage on the Mount of Olives. He sent two of His disciples ahead, instructing them to bring back to Him an ass with her colt. This was done to fulfill the prophecy: "Tell the daughter of Zion, your King comes to you without display astride an ass, astride a colt, the foal of a beast of burden." He was to enter Jerusalem as King of Peace and not as a conqueror.

Jesus enters Jerusalem in triumph.

The disciples did as Jesus told them, and then they laid their cloaks on the animal and Jesus mounted. The great crowd that had come up for the feast spread their garments on the road, while some cut down palm branches and strewed them along the way. Many of those who came out to meet Him knew that He had raised Lazarus from the dead.

113

The people kept crying out: "Hosanna to the Son of David! Blessed is He Who comes in the name of the Lord! Hosanna in the highest!" (These are the words we say at Mass after the "Holy, holy, holy.")

The Pharisees objected and asked Christ to silence the people. But Jesus answered them: "If they were to keep silence, I tell you the stones would cry out." The Pharisees were beside themselves with anger. "See, there is nothing you can do! The whole world has gone after Him," they said to one another.

Now the Passover was a great feast of the Jews, and Greeks and others who practiced Judaism also came up to Jerusalem to worship. Some of these spoke to Philip, asking to see Jesus. When Jesus heard this, He answered: "The hour has come for the Son of Man to be glorified." Then He said: "Father, glorify Your name!" Then a voice was heard from heaven: "I have glorified it, and will glorify it again." Some hearing this said it thundered, while others claimed that an angel spoke to Him.

Jesus answered them: "That voice did not come for My benefit, but for yours. Now has judgment come upon this world, now will this world's prince be driven out. But I— once I am lifted up from the earth—will draw all men to Myself." (Jesus said this to show the kind of death He was to undergo.)

As He looked over the city with its beautiful Temple and magnificent buildings, Jesus wept. "If only you had known the path to peace this day; but it is hidden from your eyes!" Then He foretold its utter destruction. He left the city that evening and returned to Bethany.

THE BARREN FIG TREE

Early the next morning Jesus was returning to Jeru-salem, and He was hungry. He came to a fig tree and finding no fruit on it, He said to it: "Never again shall you produce fruit!" Instantly it withered up.

When He entered the Temple, He again began to expel the buyers and sellers and the money-changers from the Temple. He said: "It is written, 'My house shall be called a house of prayer, but you are turning it into a den of thieves.' " Our Lord showed by this act that God's house is not to be abused and that people must be taught the real meaning of reverence and worship.

THE AUTHORITY OF JESUS

After spending the night on the Mount of Olives, Jesus and His disciples returned to the city. While He was teaching in the Temple precincts, the chief priests and the elders asked Him by what authority He did these things. (They were referring to His cleansing of the Temple.) Jesus told them in reply that if they could answer a question He would put to them, He would tell them the source of His authority. So He asked: "Was John's baptism of divine origin or merely from men?"

They knew that if they said it was divine, He would ask them why they did not believe in it. On the other hand, if they answered "merely human," they would be in trouble with the people. These men feared to lose their popularity with the people. Their answer to Jesus was: "We do not know." So Jesus told them that neither would He reveal to them by what authority He acted.

Again while He was teaching and the scribes and Pharisees were present, Jesus put a question to them: "What do you think about the Messiah? Whose Son is He?" They answered: "David's." He said to them: "Then how is it that David speaking by the Spirit calls Him 'Lord', as he does: 'The Lord said to my Lord, "Sit at My right hand until I humble Your enemies beneath Your feet?' " If David calls Him 'Lord,' how can He be his Son?" They were unable to answer Him. The majority of the crowd heard this with delight.

Then Jesus began to warn the crowd and His disciples about the hypocrisy of the scribes and Pharisees. He upheld their authority as teachers of the Law, since they were the successors of Moses. But He pointed out that they liked places of honor and to be held in high esteem, and that they did their deeds for others to see. Our Lord tells us very plainly that whoever exalts himself shall be humbled, but whoever humbles himself shall be exalted, that is, in the kingdom of heaven.

THE WIDOW'S MITE

While seated near the treasury, Jesus was watching the people dropping money into the collection box. Along came a poor widow who put in two small copper coins worth a few cents. Calling His disciples' attention to this, He told them that this poor woman had given more than all the rest; for they contributed from their surplus money, while she had given all she had to live on.

CHRIST'S SECOND COMING

Seated with His disciples on the Mount of Olives, our Lord foretold the destruction of the Temple and of the whole city of Jerusalem. Then He warned them of the coming of false prophets, and all the signs which were to precede the end of the world. No one but the Father knows the exact time of the second coming of Christ. Jesus therefore warns His followers and us of the need always to be on our guard. We must watch and pray constantly and obey His commandments. The parables of the "Ten Virgins" and the "Talents" illustrate very plainly this warning of being watchful.

THE BETRAYAL

The chief priests and the scribes were trying to find some way they could arrest Jesus and put Him to death. The Passover was drawing near and they were afraid of starting a riot among the people if they attempted to execute their plans during that time.

Satan played into their hands in the person of Judas Iscariot, one of the Twelve. He went to them and asked how much they would pay him to turn Jesus over to them; for Judas knew His whereabouts and could look for a favorable opportunity. They offered him thirty pieces of silver, and he accepted.

INSTITUTION OF THE HOLY EUCHARIST

It was customary on the first day of Unleavened Bread to sacrifice the paschal lamb. Therefore, Jesus sent Peter and John into the city to make preparations for the feast. "You will come upon a man carrying a water jar," Jesus told them. "Follow him into the house he enters, and say to the house-holder, 'The Teacher asks you: "Where is My guest room where I may eat the Passover with My disciples?" ' That man will show you an upper room, spacious and furnished. It is there you are to prepare."

They found everything as the Lord had told them and prepared the Passover supper. When they were all assembled, Jesus said to them: "I have earnestly desired to eat this Passover with you before I suffer. I tell you I will not eat again until it is fulfilled in the kingdom of God."

During the paschal supper, Jesus rose from the table, put aside His cloak, and tied a towel around Himself. He poured water into a basin and began to wash the disciples' feet. Simon Peter protested this servile act of Jesus, but Jesus assured him that if He did not wash him, he, Peter, could not share in Christ's heritage. Peter immediately agreed to be cleaned. Our Lord told them that, although He had washed all, they were not all clean. He was referring to His betrayer.

When He again reclined at table, He told the disciples that though He was their Master and Teacher, yet He had washed their feet. He was setting them an example of humility. They must do likewise to one another. What great condescension and humility the loving Heart of Jesus showed them and us! He, being God, washed the feet of lowly men!

After this, Jesus announced that one of the Twelve would betray Him. Such a thing was incredible to them, and they were very much upset. They began to question among themselves as to which one would do such a thing. Jesus told the beloved disciple, who leaned next to Him at table, that the man to whom He would give the bit of food dipped in the dish was the one. Then He dipped the morsel and gave it to Judas Iscariot. After he had eaten the morsel, Judas left. It was night.

Then our Lord took bread in His hands, gave thanks, broke it, and gave it to His disciples, saying: "This is My Body, which will be given up for you." Then He took the chalice and did the

Jesus institutes the Holy Eucharist.

same, saying: "This is the chalice of My Blood, the Blood of the new and eternal Covenant, which will be poured out for you and for many for the forgiveness of sins. Do this in memory of Me."

By the words: "Do this in memory of Me," Jesus insured that His priesthood would continue in His Church through the Apostles and their successors. He gives the dignity of a royal priesthood to all the members of His Church (called the "common priesthood of the faithful") by the Sacrament of Baptism. And from these He chooses men to share His sacred ministry by the laying on of hands in the Sacrament of Holy Orders (called the "ministerial priesthood").

"The ministerial priest, by the sacred power he enjoys, teaches and rules the priestly people; acting in the person of Christ, he brings about the Eucharistic Sacrifice, and offers it to God in the name of all the people. But the faithful, in virtue of their royal priesthood, join in the offering of the Eucharist. They likewise exercise that priesthood in receiving the Sacraments, in prayer and thanksgiving, in the witness of a holy life, and by self-denial and active charity" (Vatican II: *Constitution on the Church*, art. 10).

Thus, Christ the Lord instituted the Eucharistic Sacrifice of His Body and Blood and entrusted it to the Church, as a memorial of His Passion and Resurrection. The Lord's Supper or Mass gathers together the people of God, with a priest presiding in the person of Christ, to celebrate the memorial of the Lord or Eucharistic Sacrifice. For this reason the promise of Christ is particularly true of such a local congregation of the Church: "Where two or three are gathered together in My Name, there am I in their midst."

In the celebration of Mass, which perpetuates the sacrifice of the cross, Christ is really present in the assembly itself, which is gathered together in His Name, in the person of the minister, in His Word, and indeed substantially and unceasingly under the Eucharistic species.

After the departure of Judas and the institution of the Holy Eucharist, Jesus warned the disciples that their faith in Him was about to be shaken. Peter protested that though all might abandon Him he would not. Then Jesus solemnly told Peter that before the cock crowed he, Peter, would deny his Master three times. Christ also told Peter that though Satan would like to take Peter away from Him, He had prayed for him so that his faith would not fail and he would strengthen the others.

Before leaving the supper room, Jesus gave His disciples His new commandment of love: they must love one another as He had loved them. He also warned them of the hatred of the world, because the spirit of the world hated Him and would hate all His followers. He said they would be persecuted for His name's sake. But He also promised to send them the Holy Spirit after He returned to His Father. The Spirit of truth and holiness would be with them and His Church for all time.

Then they all sang a hymn and went out across the Kidron Valley toward the Mount of Olives.

GARDEN OF GETHSEMANE

When they reached the garden where Jesus often spent time in prayer, He took Peter, James and John with Him and asked them to watch while He prayed. He withdrew a little from them and fell prostrate in prayer: "My Father, if it is possible, allow this cup to be taken from Me. Still, let Your will, not Mine, be done." When He returned to them after His prayer, He found them asleep. He said to Peter: "Could you not keep watch with Me for even one hour?" And He exhorted them to watch and pray that they would not give in to temptation.

Jesus withdrew a second time and prayed in the same words as before. Then returning to the disciples He found them asleep once more; they could not keep their eyes open. He left them and prayed a third time, saying the words as before. An angel came from heaven to strengthen Him. Jesus experienced such anguish that His sweat became like drops of blood falling to the ground.

Our Lord Jesus shows us how important it is for us to pray in all necessities, but especially in time of temptation.

ARREST OF JESUS

Then Judas arrived with soldiers from the high priest. Going up to Jesus, he kissed Him. This was the sign he had given to the soldiers to seize Jesus and take Him prisoner. Jesus said to him: "Judas, would you betray the Son of Man

Jesus is betrayed by Judas with a kiss.

with a kiss?" How merciful was our Divine Lord with this unfortunate man. Had Judas asked for forgiveness, Jesus would have pardoned him at once.

Meanwhile, Peter drew his sword and cut off the ear of Malchus, the servant of the high priest. But Jesus told Peter to put away his sword for He must carry out His heavenly Father's will. He then healed the man's ear. When they bound

Jesus and led Him away, all the disciples fled, as He had predicted.

BEFORE ANNAS

Jesus was first brought before Annas, the father-in-law of Caiaphas who was high priest that year. Annas questioned Him regarding His disciples and His teaching. Jesus answered him that He had always spoken publicly and had taught in a synagogue or in the Temple area. Therefore Annas should question those who had heard Him. For this answer one of the guards struck Jesus across the face. Jesus' reply was: "If I have spoken wrongly, testify to My error. But if I have spoken rightly, why did you strike Me?"

PETER'S DENIAL

Meantime, Simon Peter followed Jesus, together with another disciple (probably St. John). The other disciple knew the high priest and finally brought in Peter, who was waiting outside at the gate. The servant girl who let Peter in said to him: "Aren't you one of this Man's disciples?" Peter answered that he was not. It was a cold night and the soldiers and servants were standing by a fire warming themselves, and Peter was with them. They said to Peter: "Aren't you also one of His disciples?" But Peter denied it, saying, "I am not!"

Then one, who was related to the man whose ear Peter had cut off, said to him: "Didn't I see you in the garden with Him?" Again Peter denied it, and at that moment the cock crowed. The Lord turned and looked at Peter. Then Peter remembered the warning of Jesus that before the crowing of the cock he would deny Him three times. Peter went out and wept bitterly.

BEFORE CAIAPHAS AND THE COUNCIL

Still bound, Jesus was sent by Annas to Caiaphas. Now Caiaphas was the one who had proposed to the Jews the

Jesus proclaims His divinity before the Sanhedrin.

advantage of having one man die for the people. False witnesses were brought in, but their testimonies did not agree. Finally,
the high priest asked Jesus if He had any answers to these
accusations. Jesus remained silent. Then the high priest questioned Him directly: "Are you the Messiah, the Son of the
Blessed One?"

Jesus replied: "I am; and you will see the Son of Man seated at the right hand of the Power and coming with the clouds
of heaven." At this the high priest tore his robes and accused
our Lord of blasphemy. He asked for a verdict and they all
said Jesus was guilty of death.

BEFORE PILATE

At daybreak Jesus was led to the praetorium to appear
before Pilate, the Roman governor. Pilate questioned Him,
asking Him if He were the King of the Jews. Jesus told
Pilate that His kingdom was not of this world. "So You
are a king?" Pilate asked. Jesus replied: "It is you who say I
am a king. For this was I born, and for this I came into the

world: to testify to the truth. Everyone who is devoted to the truth listens to My voice." Pilate responded, "What is truth?"

Jesus gives witness before Pilate.

Pilate did not wait for the answer. Instead he went outside to the crowd, which kept insisting that Jesus was stirring up the people throughout Judea and Galilee. As soon as Pilate learned that Jesus was a Galilean, he sent Him to Herod, under whose jurisdiction He came. Pilate had said he found no cause to accuse Jesus of any crime and was delighted to have an excuse to be rid of the case.

BEFORE HEROD

Herod was pleased to see Jesus. He had heard many reports about Him, and was hoping Jesus would perform one of His miracles for the entertainment of him and his court. But Jesus remained completely silent when questioned and accused. Herod, being angry, treated Him with contempt. He had a white robe (the fool's garment) put on Jesus and sent Him back again to Pilate. That day Herod and Pilate became friends, for before that day they were enemies. Christ became a fool for our sakes. Many of His Saints have followed His example, preferring to be thought foolish than to abandon the truth of Christ.

THE END OF JUDAS

When Judas knew that Jesus had been condemned by the chief priests, he regretted what he had done. He returned to the chief priests and elders, saying that he had done wrong in delivering up an innocent man. They replied that they were not concerned about this; it was Judas' affair. Judas flung down the thirty pieces of silver and went out and hanged himself. If only Judas, like Peter, had turned to Jesus in true repentance, how quickly he would have been forgiven.

The chief priests took the money Judas had thrown down and purchased a field as a burial place for foreigners. It is called the "Field of Blood." This fulfilled the prophecy of Jeremiah: "They took the thirty pieces of silver, the price set on His head by the people of Israel, and they used them to purchase the potter's field as the Lord had commanded me."

BEFORE PILATE A SECOND TIME

When Jesus was brought back to Pilate after Herod dismissed Him, the governor reminded the crowd of the custom that at Passover time a prisoner of their choice could be released to them. Therefore Pilate, seeking to release Jesus, offered them the choice between Him and Barabbas, a murderer. But the chief priests stirred up the people and they all cried out: "Away with this Man! Release Barabbas to us!"

Then Pilate took Jesus and had Him scourged. This is the simple statement of the four Evangelists of this most terrible act. Scourging was a most brutal punishment, reserved for slaves and criminals. Jewish law forbade giving more than forty strokes which were applied by thongs or chains studded with bone, metal, or spikes. The victim received thirteen strokes on the bare chest and twenty-six on the back. We do not know how many Jesus received in fulfillment of the prophecy of Isaiah: "I offered My back to those who beat Me."

After this, the soldiers were given freedom to treat the condemned as they wished. Our Divine Lord was surrounded by them. Stripping Him again of His clothes, they threw an old scarlet cloak around Him—a mock symbol of royalty. Then weaving a crown made of thorns, they forced it down on His head, causing the blood to flow down into His eyes. They placed a reed in His hand for a scepter and, pretending to offer homage to Him, they saluted Him: "Hail, King of the Jews!"

They kept striking Him on the head with a reed and spitting on Him. They genuflected before Him and pretended to pay Him homage. To all this our Savior submitted in silence and without complaint. In the words of Isaiah: "I did not shield My face from mocking and spitting."

BEFORE PILATE A THIRD TIME

After having Jesus clothed again in His own robes, Pilate brought Him before all the people, hoping they would be satisfied when they saw His pitiable condition. But the mob screamed: "Crucify Him! Crucify Him!"

When the people told Pilate that they had a law that Jesus should die because He claimed to be God's Son, Pilate was frightened. He brought Jesus back into the praetorium and asked Him where He came from. Jesus was silent. Pilate reminded Him that he had power to crucify Him or to set Him free. But Jesus answered: "You would have no authority over Me at all unless it had been given to you from above. Therefore, the one who handed Me over to you is guilty of a greater sin." Our Lord went to His Passion and Death in obedience to His Father's will, to atone for sin and enable us to attain eternal salvation.

Pilate was more than eager to release Jesus. But the people shouted to him: "If you release this Man, you are no Friend of Caesar." Then they said to him: "We have no king but Caesar." So Pilate, washing his hands, said to them: "I am innocent of this Man's blood. It is your responsibility." It was for fear of losing his position in the State that Pilate turned Jesus over to them to be crucified. No amount of washing could rid Pilate of that terrible act. Christ is truly King of all. His Kingdom is an eternal one. In this world He rules from the cross, and all those who would follow Him must also carry a cross.

THE CRUCIFIXION

Then they led Jesus away to be crucified. Taking up His cross, He began the long and painful journey to the Mount of Calvary (or, Skull Place). Weakened by the loss of blood and the ordeal of His trials, He fell several times under the weight of the cross. On the way they met a Cyrenian named Simon and pressed him into service to carry the cross behind our Lord. A great crowd of people followed Him, including women who mourned for Him. Jesus turned to them and said: "Daughters of Jerusalem, do not weep for Me. Weep rather for yourselves and for your children. For behold, the days are coming when people will say, 'Blessed are the barren, the wombs that never bore children and the breasts that never nursed.' Then they will begin to say to the mountains, 'Fall on us!' and to the hills, 'Cover us!' For if they do these things when the wood is green, what will happen when it is dry?"

When they came to the place called the Skull, they stripped Him of His garments and fastened Him to the cross with nails. He was crucified between two malefactors, one on His right and the other on His left. Over His head Pilate had an inscription placed, which read, JESUS THE NAZOREAN THE KING OF THE JEWS. This was written in Hebrew, Latin and Greek, so that all could read it. The chief priests objected to this, but Pilate refused to change it.

After three hours, Jesus dies on the cross.

Then the soldiers divided His clothing among them. Since the tunic was without a seam, they rolled dice for it. In this the Scripture was fulfilled: "They divide My garments among them, and for My clothing they cast lots."

The people and their leaders insulted Him and the soldiers and those crucified with Him also taunted Him. But Jesus said: "Father, forgive them, for they do not know what they are doing." One of the malefactors blasphemed Him: "Aren't You the Messiah? Save Yourself and us!" But the one to the right of Jesus said to his companion: "Have you no fear of God, since you are under the same sentence as He is? In our case, we have been condemned justly, for we are getting what we deserve for our deeds. But this Man has committed no wrong." Then turning to Jesus, he said: "Jesus, remember me when You come into Your kingdom." Jesus answered him: "Amen, I say to you, today you will be with Me in Paradise."

This "good thief" shows us the dispositions we must have to obtain forgiveness for our sins. He admitted his sins and humbly said that he was receiving just punishment for them. Then he placed his faith and confidence in the mercy of our Lord and acknowledged Him as King. There certainly was nothing about Jesus' appearance to show that He was King and had the power to forgive sins. So this man made a real act of faith.

By the cross of Jesus stood His Mother, His Mother's sister, Mary the wife of Clopas, and Mary Magdalene. When Jesus saw His Mother standing with St. John, the beloved disciple, He said to her: "Woman, behold, your son." Then He said to the disciple: "Behold, your mother." From that time on, the disciple took our Lady into his care.

As His end was drawing near, Jesus said: "I am thirsty," that the Scripture might be fulfilled. One of the soldiers put a sponge soaked in cheap wine on a reed and raised it to His lips, trying to make Him drink, thus fulfilling the words of

Psalm 69: "In My thirst they gave Me vinegar to drink." When Jesus took the wine, He said: "It is finished."

Then, with a loud cry, Jesus said: "Father, into Your hands I commend My Spirit." And bowing His head, He delivered over His Spirit. The centurion who stood on guard, seeing how Jesus cried out when He expired, said: "Truly, this Man was the Son of God!"

It was the Preparation Day of the sabbath and the leaders of the people did not want the bodies left on the cross on that sabbath, which was a solemn feast day. Therefore they asked Pilate to have the legs broken (which hastened death) and the bodies removed. When the soldiers came to Jesus, they saw that He was already dead, so they did not break His legs. However, one of the soldiers pierced His side with a lance, and blood and water immediately flowed out. All the Scriptures concerning Him had been fulfilled: "Not one of His bones will be broken;" and another passage which says: "They shall look on the One Whom they have pierced."

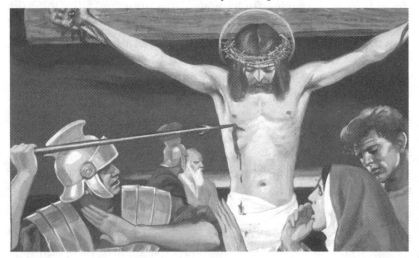

A soldier pierces Jesus' side with a lance.

Even to the end, our Divine Lord showed His great love. In his encyclical on Devotion to the Sacred Heart, Pope Pius

XII clearly states that "the wound of the Most Sacred Heart of Jesus . . . is down through the ages the living image of that love freely bestowed, by which God gave His only-begotten Son for the redemption of man, and with which Christ loved us all so intensely that He offered Himself for us as a bloody victim on Calvary." And now our Lord had clearly shown that "No one can have greater love than to lay down his life for his friends."

THE BURIAL OF JESUS

Joseph of Arimathea, a member of the Sanhedrin and a secret disciple of Jesus, together with Nicodemus, received Pilate's permission to remove the body of Jesus from the cross. They brought with them a mixture of myrrh and aloes

Jesus is taken down from the cross.

and wrapped His body with the perfumed oils in linen cloths, according to the Jewish custom of burial. There was a new tomb in the garden which was nearby. Here they laid the body of Jesus. Then they rolled a huge stone across the entrance and left. The Pharisees affixed a seal to the tomb and kept it under surveillance of their guard.

HOLY SATURDAY

While Christ's body remained in the tomb on that sabbath, His soul was in the abode where the souls of the just were awaiting the announcement of their redemption.

In the meantime, those He left on earth were grieving over His loss. This was particularly true of His Blessed Mother, although her grief was always united to faith in His Resurrection. This may be a good time for us to consider what the Church teaches us about the Blessed Virgin Mary.

Vatican Council II, in its 8th chapter in the Constitution on the Church, tells us very clearly that Mary, the Mother of the Redeemer, was "united with Him by compassion as He died on the cross. In this singular way she cooperated by her obedience, faith, hope and burning charity in the work of the Savior in giving back supernatural life to souls. Therefore she is our mother in the order of grace."

Because she is the Mother of God and united to her Son, the Blessed Virgin is also intimately united with the Church. Mary is exalted above all angels and men, by the grace of God, and therefore is rightly honored by special devotion in the Church.

Pope Paul VI, in his Apostolic Exhortation, "Devotion to the Blessed Virgin Mary," emphasizes the example of Mary's holiness as an encouragement to the faithful to look to her as a model of virtues. She, who was saluted by the angel as "full of grace," is worthy to be honored, and devotion to her "becomes for the faithful an opportunity for growing in divine grace."

The American Bishops, in their Pastoral Letter, "Behold Your Mother: Woman of Faith," show us how throughout the Gospels we are called to "recognize the special place the Mother of Jesus has in God's plan for the salvation of mankind."

Since we are dealing with Bible History, we must understand with the Church the part of Mary in Christian history. "Under the guidance of the Holy Spirit, [the Church] must preserve intact the divine message which she has received from Christ. This includes the special role of Mary in the mystery of the salvation of the human race," the Bishops continue. They then refer to the Council Fathers' use of a passage from St. Augustine, which describes Mary as "Mother of the members of Christ . . . since she cooperated out of love so that there might be born in the Church the faithful, who are members of Christ their head."

How good it is for us to go to Mary our Mother, who comforts us as only a mother can. She presents our needs to Jesus, her Son, and leads us back to Him when we stray away from Him by sin.

EASTER MORNING

Early in the morning on the first day of the week, before daylight, there was the shock of an earthquake, and the great stone in front of our Lord's tomb rolled away. The soldiers, posted on guard at the grave, fled back to Jerusalem in terror. They reported these happenings to the authorities, telling them also that when the stone rolled back, an angel appeared in dazzling white and sat upon it.

The Pharisees and scribes did not want this story to get around, and bribed the soldiers to say that they had fallen asleep and during that time the disciples came and carried away the body of Jesus. The inconsistency of such a story either did not occur to them, or it was the best they could think up at the time. If the soldiers were asleep, how could they know who had taken away the body, or if, in fact, it had been stolen at all?

Jesus rises on the third day.

APPEARANCE TO THE WOMEN

As day was dawning, the women came to the tomb bringing spices to anoint the body of the Lord, since His burial had been so hurried because of the approaching sabbath. Mary Madgalene, Mary the mother of James, Joanna and Salome were those mentioned by the Evangelists. On the way they had discussed among themselves how they were going to remove the stone. When they arrived, they found the stone rolled back. Immediately Mary Magdalene ran to tell the disciples what had happened, saying: "They have taken the Lord out of the tomb, and we don't know where they have put Him!"

An angel tells the women Jesus has risen.

In the meantime, the other women remaining at the tomb, saw two angels in dazzling garments. The women were frightened, but the angels told them to look inside the tomb. "Why do you look among the dead for One Who is alive? He is not here. He has been raised." Then the angels gave the women a message to tell the disciples and Peter that Jesus was risen from the dead and had gone ahead to Galilee, where they would see Him.

The disciples did not believe Mary Magdalene's story, but Peter and John left at once and ran to the sepulcher. John arrived first and looked into the tomb and saw the grave clothes lying on the ground; but he did not go inside. Peter came behind him and at once went inside the tomb. There he, too, saw the wrappings on the ground, but the piece of cloth which covered the head was folded and lay in a separate place. Then the beloved disciple, who arrived first, entered the tomb after Peter. He saw and he believed. Both men returned as they had come.

Meanwhile, the women hurried on their way to carry out the angels' instructions. But Mary Magdalene returned alone to the tomb after the departure of Peter and John. She stood there weeping, fearing that someone had stolen her Master's body. Then she looked into the tomb and saw the angels seated, one at the head and the other at the foot of Jesus' grave. They asked her why she was weeping. She scarcely had time to answer them when she turned and saw Jesus standing behind her. She did not recognize Him and thought He must be the gardener. Therefore she asked Him to tell her where the body of Jesus had been laid. Jesus simply said: "Mary!" And she replied to Him: *"Rabbouni"* (which means "Teacher").

After the other women had delivered their message to the assembled disciples, who did not believe their story, they returned to the sepulcher. On their way they met our Lord. He stood before them and said: "Peace!" Immediately they clung to His feet and paid Him homage. Shortly after this, the Risen Jesus appeared to Peter, the one He had appointed to be the leader of His apostles and who later was to strengthen their faith.

THE DISCIPLES AT EMMAUS

Later that same afternoon, two of His followers were walking toward Emmaus, talking over the events of the last few days. Jesus approached them and walked along with

Jesus meets two of His disciples on the way to Emmaus.

them. They did not recognize Him. He asked them what they were discussing. They were astonished that He did not know all that had been happening in Jerusalem. So He asked them to tell Him. They related all the events, even of the women who had been to the tomb, but had not found Him. Then Jesus explained Moses and the prophets to them, showing them what little faith they had. "Was it not necessary that the Messiah should suffer these things and enter into His glory?" He asked.

When they came to the village, they urged Him to stay and have supper with them. While they were eating, Jesus took bread, pronounced the blessing, broke the bread and gave it to them. At once they recognized Him in the breaking of the bread. Then He disappeared from their sight. They hurried back to Jerusalem, where they found the Eleven and the rest of the company assembled. They were greeted with, "The Lord has truly been raised, and He has appeared to Simon." Then they recounted their own experience.

APPEARANCE TO THE DISCIPLES

While they were comparing notes, Jesus came and stood in the midst of them, though the doors were locked because of their fear of the Jews. "Peace be with you," He said, and He showed them His wounds. Then He sat down and ate and drank with them to reassure them that it was really He. "Peace be with you," He repeated. "As the Father has sent Me, so I send you."

Then He breathed on them and said: "Receive the Holy Spirit. If you forgive the sins of anyone, they are forgiven. If you retain anyone's sins, they are retained." As at the Last Supper, He had given His apostles power to consecrate His body and blood in the Sacrament of the Holy Eucharist, so on the evening of His Resurrection He gave them the power to forgive sins, or to hold them bound, in the Sacrament of Penance.

Thomas was absent at this Easter Sunday meeting. When they all told him that they had seen the Lord, he refused to believe them, saying: "Unless I see the mark of the nails on His hands and put my finger into the place where the nails pierced and insert my hand into His side, I will not believe."

Jesus shows His wounds to a doubting Thomas.

Eight days later, Jesus again appeared to the disciples and this time Thomas was with them. He came despite the locked doors and said: "Peace be with you!" When our Lord showed Thomas His sacred wounds and invited him to put his finger into the nailprints and his hand into His side, Thomas cried out: "My Lord and my God!" Then Jesus said to him, "You have come to believe because you have seen Me. Blessed are those who have not seen and yet have come to believe."

CHRIST'S CHARGE TO ST. PETER

One day when several of the disciples were fishing in the Sea of Tiberias, Jesus appeared again to them. Simon Peter had announced that he was going fishing. So James and John, Thomas, Nathaniel and two others joined him. All night they had been fishing without any results. As day dawned, Jesus was on the shore, though none of the disciples knew it was Jesus. He asked them if they had caught anything. When they replied that they had not, He told them to cast their net on the right side of the ship. When they did so, they caught so many fish that they were unable to bring them to shore.

Suddenly, John said to Peter: "It is the Lord!" Immediately Peter jumped into the water and swam ashore. When the rest arrived, hauling the net full of fish, they saw a charcoal fire with a fish already cooking, and some bread. Jesus told them to bring some of the fish they had just caught. There were 153 sizable fish and yet the net was unbroken.

After Jesus had given them the bread and the fish, He turned to Simon Peter and said: "Simon, son of John, do you love Me more than these?" Simon answered: "Yes, Lord, You know that I love You." Jesus told him: "Feed My lambs." Then Jesus asked him the question again. When Peter gave Him the same answer, He said: "Tend My sheep." Then Jesus asked Peter a third time if he loved Him. Peter felt hurt, and he answered: "Lord, You know everything. You know that I love You." Jesus replied: "Feed My sheep."

Then Jesus proceeded to tell Peter that he would follow His Master to the same kind of death, for he, Peter, would stretch out his hands when he was an old man, and by this martyrdom he would glorify God.

THE ASCENSION

After forty days, Jesus led His disciples out near Bethany. He then gave them His commandment: "Go into the whole world and proclaim the Gospel to all creation. . . . Make disciples of all nations, baptizing them in the name of the Father, and of the Son, and of the Holy Spirit, and teaching them to observe all that I have commanded you. And behold, I am with you always, to the end of the world!" Then raising His hands and blessing them, He was taken up into heaven. He

Jesus ascends to heaven, leaving Mary and His disciples.

sits at the right hand of God, the Father, and continues to intercede with the Father for us. He will come again to judge the living and the dead.

There are many other things which Jesus did, as St. John tells us; but if they were all to be written down, the whole world could not contain the books that would be written. This ends the Gospel of our Lord Jesus Christ, according to the holy Evangelists Matthew, Mark, Luke and John.

Jesus Christ is not only an historical figure Who lived and worked and died 2000 years ago. He is that, of course. But He is much more: He is our God, our Savior, the One Who loves us more than anyone else. He lives now among us, as He promised.

In the words of the Second Vatican Council, "Christ is always present in His Church, especially in her liturgical celebrations. He is present in the sacrifice of the Mass, not only in the person of His minister . . . *but especially under the Eucharistic species.* By His power He is present in the sacraments so that when man baptizes it is really Christ Himself Who baptizes. He is present in His word, since it is He Himself Who speaks when the holy Scriptures are read in the Church. He is present, finally, when the Church prays and sings, for He promised: 'Where two or three are gathered together for My sake, there am I in the midst of them' " *(Constitution on the Sacred Liturgy,* no. 7).

How we must thank Him for this great gift of Himself, which He has given us! We must return His love. We do this by keeping free from sin and obeying His commandments. He loves us so much that He gives us the grace to do this, if we ask Him for it.

So we learn that the words of the "Our Father," which He taught us, is the way we adore and praise Him, the way we thank Him and love Him, and the way we ask Him for our spiritual and temporal needs, and to forgive us our sins. The same prayer also teaches us how to obey Him by forgiving those who hurt us in any way, and by working for the salvation and the good of others.

The Holy Spirit descends on the disciples at Pentecost.

ELECTION OF MATTHIAS

The Acts of the Apostles is a history of the early Church after our Lord's Ascension into heaven, written by St. Luke.

As Christ had instructed them, all the apostles and disciples waited in Jerusalem for the coming of the Holy Spirit. They spent the time in prayer, together with Mary, the Mother of our Lord. Peter, as the head of the little band, told them they should elect another apostle to take the place of Judas. So they drew lots and Matthias was chosen.

DESCENT OF THE HOLY SPIRIT

While they were all praying together on the day of Pentecost, there was a sudden noise like a strong wind blowing which could be heard throughout the house. Then there appeared tongues of fire which rested on each one of them. They were all filled with the Holy Spirit and immediately began to speak in foreign languages, as the Holy Spirit prompted them.

There were many Jews staying in Jerusalem at that time who had come from other places for the feast. When they heard the rush of wind a huge crowd gathered. Then the apostles went out and spoke to the people. They were all amazed that each one understood what was spoken in his own native tongue, for they knew these men to be simple Galileans.

Peter stood up and, beginning with the prophets, explained to them how Jesus had fulfilled all the prophecies concerning the Messiah. The people were very much impressed and asked what they must do. So Peter told them they had to reform and be baptized in the Name of Jesus Christ. About 3,000 were converted and baptized that day.

THE LAME MAN

One day when Peter and John were going into the Temple to pray, a poor cripple lay at the gate begging. The apostles saw the man, and Peter said to him: "Look at us!" The lame man did so, hoping to receive an alms. Then Peter said to him: "I have neither silver nor gold, but what I have I give you. In the Name of Jesus Christ of Nazareth, stand up and walk!" The man was cured at once and went into the Temple with them, praising God.

The people were filled with wonder when they saw what had happened. Peter spoke to those gathered in Solomon's Portico. He told them that they should not be surprised at what they had seen, for the apostles had not performed this act by their own power. He preached to them about Christ's Death and Resurrection, telling them that it was by the power of His Name that this cripple was cured.

Needless to say, the priests, the captain of the Temple guard and the Sadducees were furious. So Peter and John were put in jail for the night. But many who heard Peter talk believed. When Peter and John were taken before the Sanhedrin for questioning, Peter again spoke up, being filled with the Holy Spirit. The leaders were amazed at the speech and the fearlessness of Peter and John, knowing them to be uneducated men, but they let them go for they feared the people.

STATE OF THE CHRISTIANS

All these first Christians were of one faith and heart and they shared their belongings in common. Many sold their property and distributed everything according to the needs of each one. Every day they would pray together in the Temple, praising God. Then they would meet in their homes for "the breaking of bread," as the Eucharist was called.

ANANIAS AND SAPPHIRA

Ananias and his wife Sapphira sold a piece of property. Instead of giving all the proceeds to the apostles, as others had done, they agreed between themselves to hold out a portion of it to keep for their own use. When they laid the money at the feet of the apostles, Peter was aware that they had lied about the real value of the land. He denounced them both because they had lied to the Holy Spirit. At the sound of his words, Ananias fell dead. After this the people were filled with great fear.

HEALING THE SICK

As our Lord had promised them, the apostles worked many signs and wonders. They gathered together in Solomon's Portico each day and many more men and women came to believe in the Lord. People from Jerusalem and the towns nearby brought their sick to be healed, as well as those possessed by evil spirits. Some even laid their sick on mats in the street so that when Peter passed by at least his shadow might fall on them and make them whole.

THE APOSTLES IMPRISONED

The high priest and the Sadducees were filled with jealousy at the popularity of the apostles, as well as angered by their paying no attention to the previous order to stop preaching in the Name of Jesus. This time all of them were thrown into prison. However, during the night an angel of the Lord opened the prison gates and told them to go forth and continue to preach.

GAMALIEL

The Twelve immediately resumed their preaching. Meanwhile the full council of the elders of Israel came together and demanded that the prisoners be brought in. The Temple guard reported that when they went to the jail they found the doors locked and the guards at their posts, but no one was inside the jail. Then someone said that the men were in the Temple teaching the people.

Again the Twelve were arrested and brought before the Sanhedrin. The high priest asked them why they disobeyed the orders not to preach in Jesus' Name. Peter and the rest replied that it was better to obey God than men! They testified that Christ was at the right hand of the Father as king and Savior. The council was furious and wanted to kill them.

Then one of their number, named Gamaliel, advised them to let the Twelve alone. If their teaching is of human origin, he reasoned, it will soon disappear. On the other hand, if it comes from God, nothing they could do would destroy it and they would be going against God Himself. The Sanhedrin decided to follow Gamaliel's advice. However, before they were dismissed, the apostles were whipped. They were full of joy that they had been considered worthy to suffer for the Name of Jesus. From then on they continued preaching the Good News as our Lord had commanded them to do.

THE DEACONS

The number of Christians increased rapidly and it soon became apparent that assistants were needed to look after the daily distribution of food and the other works of service. Therefore, the apostles and disciples decided to select seven men from among their followers, who were known for their piety and wisdom, and appoint them to attend to these details. This would leave the Twelve and the disciples free to give their time to prayer and the ministry of the word. The best known of these deacons, as they were called, were Stephen and Philip. All seven men were presented to the apostles, who first prayed over them and then imposed hands on them.

STEPHEN (35 A.D.)

Stephen was filled with grace and wisdom and worked many signs among the people. Certain sects engaged him in debates, but they were no match for him. So they decided to bring up charges and called in false witnesses to say that Stephen had spoken against God and Moses. They brought him before the Sanhedrin, but he remained serene throughout their false accusations. His face was like that of an angel. Stephen then proceeded to give them a history of the Jewish people, beginning with the covenant God made with Abraham.

When he had related all these things, Stephen reproved them for their obstinacy and their pride in opposing the Holy Spirit and murdering the prophets who had foretold the coming of the Messiah. Those who heard him were furious. They dragged him out of the city and began to stone him. But Stephen prayed: "Lord Jesus, receive my spirit." His dying words were a prayer for his murderers: "Lord, do not hold this sin against them." A young man named Saul consented

Stephen the deacon is stoned to death.

to this act. After Stephen's martyrdom, the persecution of the Church spread from Jerusalem throughout all the surrounding area.

PHILIP

Philip the deacon went down to Samaria to preach the word to the people there. He performed many miracles, casting out evil spirits and curing the sick. The crowds flocked to him and listened attentively to his teaching. One of his converts was a magician named Simon Magus. This man had attracted crowds for a long time by his magic tricks. When the people began to believe in the Name of Jesus and the word of God which Philip preached to them, they were baptized. Simon, too, believed and was baptized. He was amazed by the great miracles he saw.

Later, Peter and John went down to Samaria. They prayed that the newly baptized would receive the Holy Spirit, and imposed hands on them. Now when Simon saw how they all received the Holy Spirit by the laying on of hands, he asked Peter and John to give him this power and offered them money. Peter told him to keep his money, that the gift of God could not be bought. He also told Simon to reform his life and to beg God's pardon for his evil thoughts. Simon asked them all to pray that the Lord would forgive him.

After this, an angel of the Lord told Philip to travel south to the road that went from Jerusalem to Gaza. Philip did so, and on the way he saw a man from Ethiopia, one of the Queen's court officials. This man was reading the prophet Isaiah as he was returning home from a pilgrimage to Jerusalem. Inspired by the Holy Spirit, Philip ran up ahead of the carriage. He asked the man if he understood what he was reading. The man answered Philip that he needed someone to explain it to him.

The passage he was reading concerned the Passion and Death of our Lord. Philip joined the man in his carriage and preached the Good News of Jesus to him. The man believed the word Philip spoke to him with all his heart. So when they came to some water he asked Philip to baptize him. Philip did so and then the Spirit of the Lord took Philip away. The man did not see him again, but he went on his way rejoicing.

CONVERSION OF SAUL (37 A.D.)

Meanwhile Saul carried on his persecution against the Church. He received letters from the high priest to the synagogue in Damascus, giving him the right to arrest any of the

Christians he found and bring them to Jerusalem for trial. On his way, a brilliant light suddenly flashed before his eyes. He fell to the ground and heard a voice saying to him: "Saul, Saul, why are you persecuting Me?" "Who are you, Lord?" Saul asked. And the voice replied: "I am Jesus, Whom you are persecuting." Then the voice told him to get up and go into the city, where he would be told what to do. When Paul arose and opened his eyes, he could see

Jesus appears to Saul on the road to Damascus.

nothing and had to be led into the city by those accompanying him. He remained blind for three days and neither ate nor drank.

One of the disciples in Damascus, named Ananias, received a vision from the Lord, telling him to go to the house where Saul was praying. The Lord also told Ananias that Saul was to be His chosen instrument to preach His Name to the Gentiles. Ananias did as the Lord commanded him. When he laid his hands on Saul's eyes, something like scales fell from them and Saul could see again. Ananias baptized him and Saul was filled with the Holy Spirit.

AENEAS AND TABITHA

On one of Peter's numerous journeys, he visited the holy people of God at Lydda. There was a paralytic named Aeneas who had not left his bed for eight years. Peter told him: "Aeneas, Jesus Christ heals you. Get up and make your bed." The man was cured at once. All who saw the miracle were converted.

Then Peter went to Joppa, where a woman named Tabitha fell sick and died. She was well known for her many charitable deeds. When Peter was informed of her death, he went at once to the house where the woman was laid out. He knelt beside the body and prayed. Then he said: "Tabitha get up." She opened her eyes, looked at Peter and sat up. He called in the Christians and presented her alive.

CORNELIUS

In Caesarea lived a Roman centurion named Cornelius. He and all his household were God-fearing people. He prayed to God continually and gave alms to all in need. While he was praying one day, an angel appeared to him and told him that his prayers and his generosity were pleasing to God.

Then the angel said that he should send for Peter, who lodged with a tanner by the sea. Cornelius sent some of his servants to Joppa.

Peter had a vision while he was praying on the rooftop: a large canvas-like object descended from the sky, in which were all kinds of animals, reptiles and fowl. A voice told him to kill and eat. Peter replied that he had never eaten anything unclean. Then the voice said: "What God has made clean you must not call profane." While Peter was trying to understand the meaning of the vision, the messengers from Cornelius arrived asking for him. Peter immediately went down, listened to their story and went with them to Caesarea.

When they arrived at Cornelius' house, he had gathered together his relatives and special friends. Peter spoke to all present, telling them about our Lord's life, Death and Resurrection. He said that the apostles were witnesses to the Resurrection and that our Lord had commanded them to preach the Good News, and to bear witness that He is the judge of the living and the dead. After Peter's instruction, the gift of the Holy Spirit was given to the Gentiles, and they were baptized in the Name of Jesus Christ.

PETER'S DELIVERANCE

King Herod Agrippa began to persecute the Church about this time. He beheaded James, the brother of John. This pleased the Jews, so Herod proceeded to put Peter into prison. Since the Passover was drawing near, Peter was put in the custody of four squads of soldiers. It was Herod's intention to bring Peter before the people after the feast. Continuous prayer was offered for him by the Church.

Peter was sleeping between two soldiers, fastened with double chains, while guards watched at the door. Suddenly a light shone in the cell and an angel stood by him. Striking Peter on the side, the angel told him to get up, dress himself and follow him. Peter thought he was seeing a vision. They passed through the guards and came to the iron gate leading out to the city. This opened of itself and they passed on through to the street. There the angel left Peter, who realized where he was. "Now I am positive," he said, "that the Lord has sent His angel and rescued me from Herod's clutches and from all that the Jewish people were expecting."

When Peter came to the house where the Christians were gathered together in prayer, he knocked at the door. When Rhoda saw that it was Peter, she ran back to tell the others, who could scarcely believe her. They were overjoyed at seeing him and knew that their prayer had been answered through the ministry of God's angel.

HEROD'S DEATH

Herod had a search made to find Peter and when this proved futile he had the guards executed. Then he went to Caesarea. Herod was angry with the people of Tyre and Sidon. They presented themselves before him in court in order to make peace with him because their countries received food supplies from Herod. When Herod spoke to them, the people acclaimed him a god and not a man. Because he did not give the honor to God, the angel of the Lord struck him down at once and he died eaten by worms.

PAUL'S FIRST JOURNEY (44/45)

There was a group of prophets and teachers in the Church at Antioch. While they were celebrating the liturgy and fasting, the Holy Spirit made known to them that He had chosen Saul and Barnabas for a special mission. After they had fasted and prayed, they imposed hands on them and sent them off. The two went to Seleucia, and sailing from there they came to Cyprus. They proclaimed the word throughout the island as far as Paphos. The proconsular governor there sent for Barnabas and Saul (also known as Paul), as he was eager to hear the word of God.

But there was a Jewish magician, a false prophet, attached to the governor's court, who opposed the apostles and tried to dissuade the governor from accepting the faith. Paul denounced this evil man and exposed him as a fraud. Calling him a son of Satan, Paul told him that he would be blind because of his blasphemy. Immediately a mist of darkness came upon him and he groped for someone to lead him. When the governor saw what had happened, he believed the teaching about the Lord.

Paul and Barnabas then set sail for Antioch and entered the synagogue there on the sabbath. After the reading of the Law and the Prophets, they were invited to speak. Paul arose and, reminding his listeners of the Savior that was promised, preached the word of salvation to them. He told them of the Death and Resurrection of our Lord, and that through Him only is forgiveness of sins. Many were impressed with his words and were converted.

When some of the Jews saw the great number of converts, they were envious and tried to contradict what Paul had said. Then Paul and Barnabas denounced them for their unbelief and turned to preach the word to the Gentiles, many of whom became converts. After this, the angry Jews forced them to leave the city. So they shook the dust of that place from their feet in protest and went on to Iconium.

In Iconium they converted a number of Jews and Greeks. A division of opinion over their teaching broke out among the people, and the leaders threatened to stone them. When Paul and Barnabas heard this, they fled to Lystra, where they cured a man crippled from birth. When the crowd saw this, they wanted to offer sacrifice to them as gods. But the apostles assured them that they were only men like themselves.

Some of their enemies came from Antioch and Iconium and aroused the people against Paul and Barnabas. Then they stoned Paul and dragged him out of the city, where they left him thinking he was dead. The two, however, returned to

Antioch and related all that God had accomplished through them, even to the conversion of the Gentiles to the faith.

COUNCIL OF JERUSALEM (49 A.D.)

Since a controversy arose between some of the brothers and Paul and Barnabas concerning circumcision for Gentile converts, it was decided that they should go to Jerusalem and take up this matter with the apostles and the Church assembled. There was much disputing among them until Peter rose up and spoke. He reminded them of how the Gentiles had believed the word of God and that the Holy Spirit had been given to them as well as to the Jews. Then they all remained silent while Paul and Barnabas told them about their mission.

After that, James, who was then Bishop of Jerusalem, agreed that the Gentiles should not be burdened with circumcision, but that a decree of the apostles be sent to them— to be delivered by Paul and Barnabas—instructing them that they must refrain from all their former pagan ways and serve God faithfully. This was the first council of the Church.

PAUL'S SECOND JOURNEY (50-52 A.D.)

On this journey Paul took Silas as his companion, while Barnabas sailed for Cyprus, taking Mark with him. At Lystra, Paul and Silas met Timothy, a disciple whose mother was a Jewess and a believer, and whose father was Greek. Timothy was highly respected among the brothers in that place, and Paul took him along on the journey as well. The churches already established grew stronger in faith and daily increased in numbers.

While visiting Troas, Paul had a vision in which a man of Macedonia was inviting him to come there and help them. So they sailed from Troas and arrived in Philippi, a leading city of Macedonia. There they preached to a group of women gathered together on the sabbath. One of them, a devout woman named Lydia, accepted their teaching and invited Paul and his companions to stay at her house. She and her whole household were baptized.

From there Paul and Silas went to Thessalonica, where Paul preached to the Jews assembled at the synagogue. Many of the Jews and Greeks were converted. This aroused the anger of the Jews, so at night when the disturbance was over, Paul and Silas left for Beroea where they made numerous converts among both the Jews and influential Greeks. Again trouble was stirred up and Paul set out to sea for Athens. Later Silas and Timothy joined him there.

In Athens, Paul saw idols everywhere. He held discussions with some of the popular philosophers of the day. These people were always looking for new ideas, so they invited Paul to speak to them about his doctrine. Paul told them they were superstitious and pointed out an altar they had dedicated "To a God Unknown." He preached to them about the one true God, advising them of the day when God would judge the world. A few, including Dionysius, a member of the court, and a woman named Damaris, were converted.

Leaving Athens, Paul next came to Corinth. Here he earned his living by his trade of tent-making. He preached to the Jews there and was joined by Silas and Timothy. There was so much opposition to his teaching that Paul left them and turned his attention to the Gentiles. Paul remained in Corinth for over a year converting and baptizing many of the Corinthians, including Titus and Crispus. Leaving Corinth, Paul went to Ephesus. He did not remain there long, but promised to return. He went on to Caesarea, where he visited the Christian congregations. Then he continued traveling through Galatia and Phrygia, encouraging all his disciples.

PAUL'S THIRD JOURNEY (53-58 A.D.)

As he had promised, Paul returned to Ephesus. Here he found a group of converts and he asked them if they had received the Holy Spirit. They said that they knew nothing about the Holy Spirit and had been baptized with John's baptism. Paul taught them about our Lord, and they were baptized in the Name of the Lord Jesus. Then, imposing hands on them, he confirmed them and they received the Holy Spirit. Paul and his companions remained in Ephesus about two years. During that time the Gospel was preached to all the inhabitants, both Jews and Greeks, and many were converted. God also worked great miracles through Paul.

From Ephesus Paul went to Macedonia to visit the Christians and encourage them in their faith. Then he and Luke traveled to Philippi and from there to Troas, where they met their other companions. A young boy named Eutychus fell from a third-story window and was dead when they picked him up. Paul restored him to life. It was a Sunday and they all gathered together to celebrate the Eucharistic Sacrifice.

Paul made several stops on his way back to Jerusalem, establishing many churches and ordaining priests. He instructed the leaders of the Church in Ephesus to keep watch over themselves and the flock given them to guard by the Holy Spirit. He warned them against false teachers who would come even from among their own numbers. Then they all knelt down and prayed together and Paul went on his way.

When Paul and his disciples arrived in Jerusalem, they visited James and the other elders of the Church and received a warm welcome. A riot broke out in the Temple when some Jews from Asia, recognizing Paul, stirred up the crowd. He was accused of teaching against their law and profaning their sacred places. Paul tried to calm the people, but they shouted out: "Kill him!" After being imprisoned, he appeared before the Sanhedrin and was then sent to Caesarea. There he was brought before the governor, but he insisted that as a Roman citizen he be allowed to make his appeal to the Emperor.

PAUL'S JOURNEY TO ROME (61-63 A.D.)

The decision was made to send Paul to Rome where he could plead his case before Caesar. During the journey to Rome a severe storm arose which raged for several days. All on board were convinced they were lost, but Paul told them to keep up their courage. He said that though they would be shipwrecked on an island all would be safe and eventually reach their destination. Finally, they arrived in Rome and were greeted there by some of their fellow Christians. Paul was put under guard and kept in chains, but was permitted to have his own living quarters.

Here he gave witness before the Jews concerning the reign of God, trying to persuade them about Jesus through the Law of Moses and the prophets. Some were convinced, but others were not. He remained in his lodgings for two years, receiving all who came to him and writing letters to the other churches he had established, warning them against errors and encouraging them in their faith. He preached the kingdom of God to those who visited him and taught them about our Lord Jesus Christ with complete confidence and without restraint.

SECOND ROMAN CAPTIVITY AND DEATH (67 A.D.)

After two years of restraint Paul, in the year 63, was free to travel again. The Acts of the Apostles has no more to say of him, but it appears from the last letters (Titus, 1 and 2 Timothy), written between 65 and 67, that he journeyed to Crete, Asia Minor, and Greece.

In the Epistle to the Romans Paul expresses his plans for going to Spain, but it is not known if he completed this journey. He was imprisoned a second time in Rome and condemned to death. Tradition tells us that he was martyred on the Ostian Way by being beheaded during the persecution of Nero in 67 or 68 A.D.

THE CHURCH IN ADVERSITY

From the time of Nero's persecution a series of evils seem to follow one after another: epidemics, and civil wars on the part of some nations revolting against the Roman yoke.

For the Christians already frightened by the persecution of Nero, things seem to get worse every day, because paganism does not resign itself to disappear and fights with all its might.

Around the end of the first century, Domitian becomes the Emperor of Rome. One of the measures adopted by him is to oblige his subjects, under the pain of death, to offer homage of adoration to him. When the Christians refuse to do so, they are again persecuted unto death.

In the midst of the persecution, John, exiled to the island of Patmos in Turkey, writes a book in which he tries to instill hope in the hearts of the Christians. Once again the Word of God, through one of His apostles, illumines the lives of the followers of Christ.

This is the Book of Revelation. It is written in an "apocalyptic" style popular at the time. That is why the message it conveys is wrapped in images and symbols.

Some books of the Old Testament are also written in this style. They foretell evils, calamities, and persecutions that would befall the Chosen People, caused by the enemies of the Kingdom of God. But suddenly the Day of Yahweh will come and bring peace and happiness.

The last book of the New Testament, and of all the Scriptures, teaches a last lesson: the Church of Christ lives in hope; it carries a great desire in its heart: the "Parousia," that is, "the second coming of the Lord."

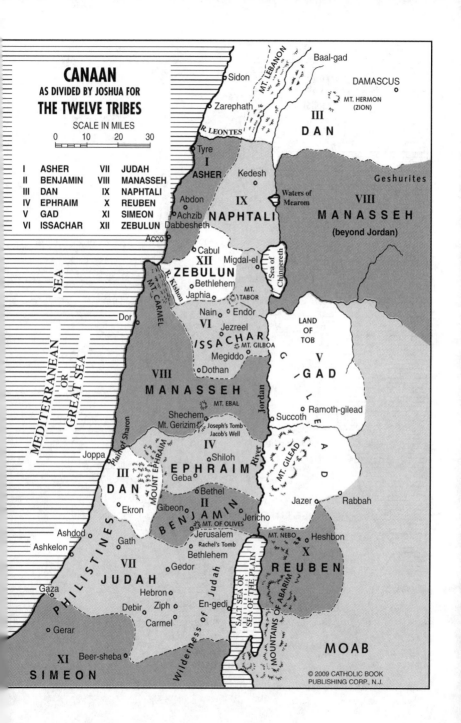

CANAAN
AS DIVIDED BY JOSHUA FOR
THE TWELVE TRIBES

SCALE IN MILES
0   10   20   30

I   ASHER   VII   JUDAH
II   BENJAMIN   VIII   MANASSEH
III DAN   IX   NAPHTALI
IV   EPHRAIM   X   REUBEN
V   GAD   XI   SIMEON
VI   ISSACHAR   XII   ZEBULUN

Baal-gad

DAMASCUS

Sidon

Zarephath

MT. LEBANON

MT. HERMON
(ZION)

R. LEONTES

III
DAN

Tyre

I
ASHER

Kedesh

Geshurites

Waters of
Mearom

Abdon

IX

VIII
M A N A S S E H

Achzib
Dabbesheth

NAPHTALI

(beyond Jordan)

Acco

Cabul

Migdal-el

SEA

XII

Sea of
Chinnereth

ZEBULUN

R. Kishon

Bethlehem

Japhia

MT.
TABOR

MT. CARMEL

Dor

Nain

Endor

VI

Jezreel

LAND
OF
TOB

Nain

I S S A C H A R

MT. GILBOA

MEDITERRANEAN
OR
GREAT SEA

Megiddo

V

VIII

Dothan

GAD

M A N A S S E H

MT. EBAL

Jordan

Plain of Sharon

Shechem

Ramoth-gilead

Joppa

Mt. Gerizim

Joseph's Tomb
Jacob's Well

Succoth

MT. GILEAD

IV

III

MOUNT EPHRAIM

Shiloh

DAN

E P H R A I M

Geba

Ekron

Bethel

Gibeon

II

Jazer

Rabbah

Ashdod

B E N J A M I N

Jericho

Gath

MT. OF OLIVES

MT. NEBO

Heshbon

Ashkelon

Jerusalem

Rachel's Tomb

River Jordan

Bethlehem

X

VII

Gedor

R E U B E N

Gaza

J U D A H

Hebron

MOUNTAINS OF ABARIM

Debir

Ziph

En-gedi

SALT SEA OR SEA OF THE PLAIN

Carmel

Gerar

PHILISTINES

Wilderness of Judah

MOAB

XI

Beer-sheba

SIMEON

© 2009 CATHOLIC BOOK
PUBLISHING CORP., N.J.

PALESTINE
IN THE TIME OF CHRIST

0   10   20
Miles

Sidon

Zarephath

R. Leontes

Tyre

PHOENICIA

MT. LEBANON

DAMASCUS

MT. HERMON

Caesarea Philippi

Paneas

Iturea

Batanea

Trachonitis

UPPER GALILEE

Chroazin

Capernaum

Magdala

Bethsaida

SEA OF GALILEE

Gaulanitis

Auranitis

Cana

Nazareth

Tiberias

MT. TABOR

Gamala

MEDITERRANEAN SEA

MT. CARMEL

LOWER GALILEE

Dor

Plain of Esdraelon

Jezreel

Gadarenes

Gadara

Caesarea

River Jordan

DECAPOLIS

SAMARIA

Samaria

Sychar

MT. EBAL

Jacob's Well

MT. GERIZIM

Gerasa

Joppa

PEREA

BEYOND THE JORDAN

Arimathea

Lydda

Ephraim

Philadelphia

Jericho

MT. OF OLIVES

JERUSALEM

Bethany

Bethlehem

Azotus

Ashkelon

JUDAH

Hebron

Judah

DEAD SEA

Machaerus

R. Arnon

Gaza

Engedi

Wilderness of

Masada

Beer-sheba

© 2009 CATHOLIC BOOK
PUBLISHING CORP., N.J.